THE
Archive Photographs
SERIES

HAVERFORDWEST

Children from Prendergast Junior School leaving Haverfordwest station for a visit to Bristol Zoo in 1962 – the school's centenary year. The group includes members of the staff: Miss Margaret Watkins, Mr Ken Thomas and Mr Walter Thomas.

THE Archive Photographs SERIES
HAVERFORDWEST

Compiled by
Haverfordwest Civic Society

CHALFORD

First published 1997
Copyright © Haverfordwest Civic Society, 1997

The Chalford Publishing Company
St Mary's Mill, Chalford,
Stroud, Gloucestershire, GL6 8NX

ISBN 0 7524 0719 8

Typesetting and origination by
The Chalford Publishing Company
Printed in Great Britain by
Redwood Books, Trowbridge

Cover picture: Boys lined up across Dew Street for the start of the Haverfordwest Grammar School annual cross-country run, 29 March 1928. The race, in which the turnout was voluntary, marked the opening of the sports season. The winner received a silver cup and ten points for his house in the school sports. On this occasion, thirty-four boys ran the seven-mile course, much of it cross country: Portfield – Dreenhill – Denant – Bolton Hill – Johnston Mill Farm – Dredgeman Hill and finally by road back to Dew Street where final placings were decided by some determined sprinting.

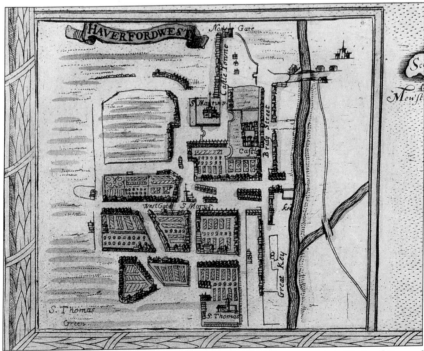

Dated 1680, this plan of Haverfordwest is from Law's *The History of Little England Beyond Wales*.

Contents

HAVERFORDWEST CELEBRITIES AS SEEN BY "MATT"

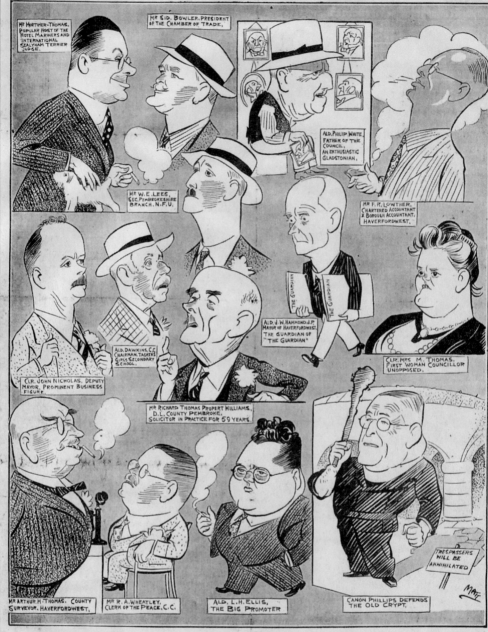

Here are some of the leading citizens of Haverfordwest as seen by Matt, our cartoonist, during his visit to the town. We leave it to readers to judge how well he has "caught" them.

Foreword

By Gerald Oliver, Chairman, Haverfordwest Civic Society

There are places that seem to inspire an intensity of affection from their inhabitants that can seem irrational to an outsider, unless he or she also succumbs to the enchantment. Haverfordwest is such a place where affection for the historic town is rendered poignant by the fact that such sweeping and often destructive changes have taken place in the last two decades, and no doubt the havoc wreaked upon the town's physical structure is a powerful factor in creating the intense interest so many people feel in the town's past, especially the past that lies within living memory.

This book, with its extensive collection of photographs of Haverfordwest, will, we hope, both stir many memories and excite curiosity. Most of the photographs have not previously been published, and we have been lucky in the unstinting and generous help we have received from so many people who have made material available to us, which we hope to share with as many people as possible.

Despite the changes of recent years, the ancient core of the town remains largely intact with its splendid High Street, crowned by St Mary's church, still looking as handsome as any street in Wales, and the domination of this river town by its Norman castle is as evident as ever. We hope our book celebrates the tenacity and resilience of this town and its people as it looks forward to the Millennium.

This photograph was taken to Prendergast Junior School in 1980 by a pupil who said it had belonged to a local lady then in her nineties. Efforts have been made by the town's Civic Society to trace the original but without success. It shows Haverfordwest in 1859 as a busy and thriving port. A close inspection reveals the name of one of the ships, the John Deer; bales of wool being unloaded; and a lady wearing a crinoline dress walking along the quayside. Inscribed on the photograph were 'Bristol Trader' and 'New Quay' and on its mount the words 'The Mayor was an "Admiral" in those days'.

Introduction

By Wyn Jones JP, FRIBA,
founder member of the Haverfordwest Civic Society and former Chairman

In recent years the townscape of Haverfordwest has suffered more than its fair share of change. Changes, less dramatic, perhaps, have also taken place in the social fabric of the town, but, seen over a span of years these have probably been more significant.

Haverfordwest Civic Society in compiling and researching this remarkable collection of photographs has enabled another publication recording the history of our town. 'Every picture tells a story', the old advert assured us. How true, and what stories!

Old photographs, apart from giving sheer enjoyment, record these changes for us. There is something in them for everyone: the pleasure of nostalgia for townspeople; historical records and references for historians and institutions; astonishment and often amusement for the young at earlier generations' way of life; styles for the fashion conscious; and for the conservationist a glimpse of buildings that should never have been demolished. The changes to the street scene have largely taken place in what the Americans picturesquely call 'the twilight zone' – that ring of often run-down streets between the historic town core and the more recent and well-maintained suburban estates. This has resulted in a very different scale of highway, due entirely to the twentieth-century phenomenon of motor traffic. The photographs record much of what has been swept out of the way.

Fortunately, the historical town remains largely intact but here, too, photographs reveal earlier buildings whose successors have been inappropriate in scale, design or finish, to the detriment of the street picture. The vernacular building tradition of Haverfordwest, like its vernacular speech, has been a victim of the twentieth century. There are many lessons here to be learnt by architects, developers, councillors and planners. No longer is the town the tightly knit community it was earlier this century. Its institutions – churches, chapels, courts, schools, local government, ceremonial events, shops, art and sporting societies – have all been caught up in the wind of change. This reflects either greater prosperity and greater mobility, or an altered pattern of shopping and living resulting from the move out of the town centre over the past fifty years.

An earlier way of life is recorded here in these frozen moments in time. But time does not stand still and the process of change continues relentlessly.

The Old Bridge, Fishguard Arms and New Inn, c. 1900.

One

Early Days

All the photographs in this section reflect the way of life in Haverfordwest when work and leisure were linked to pedestrian man and animal. Life in the town was influenced by the countryside seasons and the produce of the land. The tides timed the work on the quays and in the riverside warehouses. The coming of the railway could not speed up the day-to-day street life. The pictures in this section show Haverfordwest as a country market town at the end of the nineteenth century and in the early part of the twentieth century.

The most influential feature of a modern town is absent from these photographs – the motor car has not yet arrived. The town shown is not a place where anonymous people dash through the streets in isolation from their fellow man. This is a town where a stranger at the Salutation Square would be quite well known by the time he reached St Mary's church.

Although many fine and interesting buildings have been removed mainly to accommodate motor traffic, it is heartening to see how many remain. It would be nice to think that if any person portrayed were transported forward in time to the present day and to the spot where they were photographed, they would know they were in 'Harfat'.

Mostyn Lewis

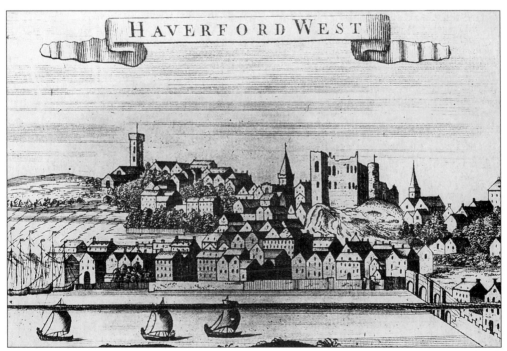

Haverfordwest in Tudor times. The castle is still more or less complete (Cromwell did not arrive until 1648), the town still has its walls, there are vineyards below St Thomas's church, and St Mary's still has its spire.

Local photographer Seth Griffiths caught this glorious image of Picton Place at the turn of the century, and what incident it shows! A horse-drawn trap carries a family past a surprisingly well-dressed man driving his six pigs, which in turn are passing another trap whose driver has allowed his horse to drink at the trough which was then sited in the centre of Salutation Square. The young trees with their protective railings contribute to a sense of urban neatness and pride.

Old High Street, with the fine new post office built in 1880. This photograph taken a little later shows the lower building occupied by workmen, with pickaxes in the middle window, presumably in the process of gutting and remodelling. The arched basement entrance looks as if it may lead into a barrel vault (as found below Swales Music Centre), but the feature is not identifiable today.

One of the earliest photographs of the town shows the upper part of High Street about 1860 with a late medieval timber-framed building that was to be demolished when the post office was built in 1880. The two buildings to the left still remain recognisable today as Swales Music Centre, despite the loss of the eighteenth-century bow windows which were such a feature of the old town.

An early nineteenth-century drawing (with its companion below), showing the south side of High Street with various bow and dormer windows that survived even into the present century. It is legitimate to speculate that these two pictures may originally have been penned by Mr Thomas Ellis of Short Row School whose well-known 1822 drawing of the street was published by his son Edmund Henry Ellis sixty-four years later

This superb early nineteenth-century drawing shows the Guildhall with its splendid gates and piers as well as three timber-framed houses, the lower two of which still exist in much reduced form. The viewpoint is from an upper window of one of the houses demolished c. 1880 to make way for the post office. The only other view of the Guildhall known at present is the celebrated lithograph, published in 1886, from Thomas Ellis's 1822 drawing of High Street.

Mounted Yeomanry crossing the New Bridge from Picton Place to Victoria Place c. 1914. Lewis's Furnishing Warehouse, established in 1832, was later the site of the County Theatre, which in turn was demolished in early 1980, and is now occupied by Pembrokeshire County Council offices. It was from the New Bridge that spectators of the 'Destructive Fire' in 1906 (below) took their 'snapshots'.

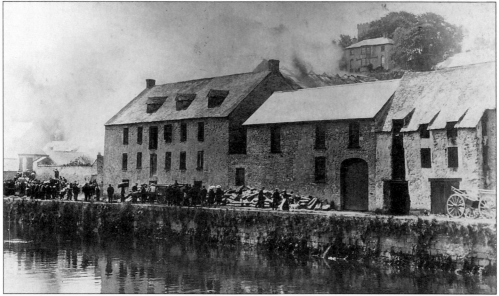

'Destructive Fire In Haverfordwest – Grocery Stores Completely Gutted'. On 27 July 1906 at about 11 o'clock in the morning, the grocery stores on the New Quay occupied by Mr Edgar W. Rees, High Street, were destroyed. The building was full of sugar, flour, and general groceries of a very inflammable nature. Within an hour the fire had burned itself out leaving only four blackened walls though it smouldered for several days. 'Quay Street and the New Bridge were soon crowded with people anxious to get a glimpse of the fire and some snap-shot views of the burning pile were taken'. The adjoining buildings were threatened for a period – stores belonging to Mr Fred Green and the residence of Mr Joseph Thomas. The old summer-house which stood at the corner of Potters Lane before the post office development can be clearly seen. Hermons Hill House and St Thomas's church are still prominent landmarks and part of the old quayside buildings can still be recognised.

Harries's Stores, *c.* 1900. Some bits of medieval building are still visible in the upper stories.

Hay makers cut hay and sharpen their scythes in this photograph of 1884 which comes from the album of George Leader Owen of Withybush. Interesting detail abounds: the large number of lime-washed buildings (including Rock House), the height of some of the Hill Street houses on the skyline, the unwalled Pyx Parade and, below that, the outline of Perrots Road and the area of the Goose Meadow where Llewellin's Churnworks had been established in 1789. No more evocative photograph of the nineteenth-century town exists.

The original Pembrokeshire South African War Memorial was unveiled on 21 October 1904. It had first been suggested by the High Sheriff, Dr Henry Owen, in 1903 and as it was to be the County Memorial it was proposed that it should be in the county town. The Town Council offered the site of the old Guildhall, an open area in a prominent position in the High Street below St Mary's church. Over many years the Cornish stonework deteriorated, until in 1986 it had to be replaced by a new cross on the original plinth. To replace it in the original design would have cost £20,000. The Royal British Legion, Preseli Pembrokeshire District Council and the Haverfordwest Town Council shared the cost of £3,000 to provide a new memorial of rustic granite in a simpler and smaller design.

Supposedly sited between Bridge Meadow Lane at the end of the Old Bridge and Bland's old garage at the bottom of Prendergast, an area which disappeared c. 1987 during the road and Riverside Quay developments. The men have a distinctive appearance – perhaps Irish – which is further emphasised by the flat-hatted priest on the extreme left and the man wearing jodhpurs close by.

A dog wheel in a Goat Street house. The wheel fitted into a recess in the wall was worked by a dog to turn the spit.

HAY RAKES for the Present Season, 1872.

No. 1, to Rake 6 feet £7 0 0
No. 2, Do. 7 feet £7 15 0
If with Steel Teeth 10s. 6d. extra.

MARYCHURCH & DAW,
MANUFACTURERS,
BRIDGE STREET, HAVERFORDWEST.

A late nineteenth-century advertisement for agricultural machinery.

16

Two

Street Scenes

It would be fascinating to have many more drawings, prints and paintings of Haverfordwest that pre-date photography and yet, valuable as they would be, the artifice of the artist must necessarily lack the innocent truthfulness of old, and not so old, photographs. The camera has been unique in its ability to catch the appearance of a place, to freeze its inhabitants for a split second, as they go about their lives. Street scenes tell us about the physical appearance of the town over the years and also tell us how our forebears lived, worked and transported themselves and, in the more recent pictures, how we and our neighbours still do. The detail fascinates: we see a policeman taking a note, one foot resting on the lost Salutation Square horse-trough (page 21); a solitary elderly lady walks along Victoria Place at the time of the Coronation (page 22), an archaic 'Town' bus crossing the Castle Square behind, and the lost Victorian detail that made the Pearl office so conspicuous, across the road. I wonder what she was thinking?

Gerald Oliver

Tower Hill and St Mary's church from the Mariners Square in 1946. The car, a 1937 two and a half litre MG model WA, parked on the hill, was owned by Mr Edgar Williams, the solicitor, whose office was in Tower Hill. Outside the Hotel Mariners is an Alvis 12/50 owned by local businessman Mr David George, a partner in the family firm, W.H. George and Son.

This evocative portrait of decaying traditional buildings behind Bridge Street *c.* 1970 vividly illustrates the problems the old town still faces, though many other buildings have been restored in recent years as the value of old buildings has been increasingly appreciated.

'The Hole in the Wall' in Bridge Street and the site of the Boys' British School between 1846 and 1859 with the old school clock still visible in this photograph. It is also remembered as the rear of Dickenson's butchers shop.

Cambrian Place before the Freemans Way by-pass opened in 1976. The garage workshop, left, was operated by Mr Fred Thomas, Trafalgar Square, Prendergast.

This part of old Haverfordwest, the entrance to Cartlett and the brook alongside, disappeared in the 1970s when the streets in the area were completely revolutionised to accommodate the ever-increasing volume of traffic. Cartlett Brook in the foreground was diverted and the buildings behind, including those of Mr Shearn's boot and shoe repair business and Clarke's grocery shop on the corner, were demolished. The bulldozer also made short work of the little newspaper and confectionery shop opposite Clarke's (run for many years by Mr Rees Howells) and within a short time all the buildings behind, including the Mill Inn, a popular rendezvous in its day, also came down. In the far background is the outline of Haverfordwest castle and, nearer, the Masonic Hall and the raised part of the old County Theatre.

Jeremy's Garage, previously Holloway's, at the Salutation Square near the entrance to Scotchwells. These buildings together with the War Memorial, have been changed or removed to accommodate road alterations.

The entrance to Cartlett showing some of the old Salutation Square buildings, including the re-located Cenotaph. This was a familiar street scene before the roads revolution transformed the Salutation Square c. 1963. Of special interest is the typically 1930s period 'lighthouse' surmounting Green's Motors filling station, long demolished but a stylish feature in its day.

Chalfont House, seen here pre-1963, was a doctor's residence and surgery for many years, with adjoining business and residential premises.

Horse drinking-trough in Salutation Square, pre-1963.

During the Christmas period 1949 and before the cobbles were removed from in front of the Shire Hall. Car parking was not a problem then and High Street was open to two-way traffic. The Commer lorry – ADE 305 – pulling away from the traffic lights still has a headlight cover fitted, a wartime blackout precaution. The traffic lights were installed in 1935 and those who failed to observe them were soon going through the courts. The fine for failing to comply with the lights was usually 2/6. One defendant caught riding his bicycle through the lights claimed he thought they were only for vehicles and motor cycles. The offence was committed at a busy time – 5 o'clock, the tea hour – and he was fined 2/6.

The Castle Hotel decorated with flowers and banners to mark the coronation in June 1953 of Queen Elizabeth II. Parked outside the Pearl Assurance office is a Standard Vanguard – SDE 920.

A corner of the Castle Square on a quiet day *c.* 1964, showing the Pearl Assurance office with its added elaborate Victorian details. The building was later replaced.

The Gay Heart Restaurant, 10 Victoria Place, in the 1950s. A popular meeting place owned by Mr and Mrs John Crowley, it is now the site of the Halifax Building Society. Mr Crowley produced the early productions by the Haverfordwest Dramatic Society.

Old cottages in Quay Street *c.* 1932 before demolition for the new post office. For many years they belonged to the Philipps family of Picton and when they were sold to Mr W.B.W. John in 1928 they were described as 'ruined cottages'. The tall buildings remain and the end wall (of No 10) is emblazoned with a large shiny boot advertising shoe repairs.

Traffic in Haverfordwest's busy High Street came to a standstill during 1980-81 when essential structural repairs and renovations were carried out at business premises on both sides of the road. The scaffolding on the left stands against Messrs Loosemore's television, radio and electrical goods shop, while the buildings affected opposite include the so-called 'Old Surgery' where a well-known firm of doctors carried on general practice for many years. An elderly resident recalling the 1920s remembered Dr Mills as a 'nice gentle man' and Dr Wilson as 'also a nice man but looked large enough to frighten any child'.

Quay Street, still with two-way traffic *c.* 1970. The new post office has replaced the ruined cottages. It was opened on 25 June 1936 by former Liberal MP Sir Evan Jones, Lord Lieutenant of Pembrokeshire. It is reported to have cost £17,000 and was 'built on the most modern principles. It is an imposing frontage without however the frontal impressiveness of the old post office in High Street'.

The flavour of ancient Haverfordwest is captured in this photograph of Lower Quay Street taken in the late 1940s. Quay Street was formerly one of the most active streets in the town, a centre of coastal trading where small ships arrived on practically every tide bearing grain, coal and a variety of business and household goods to maintain the generally high standard of town life. Many changes have been made in Quay Street, which is now almost unrecognisable compared with the days when it was so dependant on its connection with the sea. Quay Street's reputation has now changed drastically; in the old days due to its strong sea-faring associations it was an area which the honest citizens visited with apprehension, but those times have long disappeared and Quay Street is now one of our most popular and respectable thoroughfares.

The proliferation of the motor car is graphically illustrated in these two scenes of St Thomas Green. In March 1954 The Green is still an open uncluttered space with only about twenty vehicles on view and the old buildings on the right are reminiscent of the Haverford of old. By 1996 the car had taken over practically every space and the picturesque buildings on the right had been replaced by a modern residential block. This is how we have progressed!

Rosemary Lane *c.* 1960.

Hill House College in Hill Street was one
of the most successful of the many private
schools in Haverfordwest before the 1944
Education Act. It was founded by a Mrs
Philpotts, and soon acquired a high
reputation as a centre of learning and
culture, which was fully maintained after it
was taken over at about the turn of the
century by the Misses Mildred and Agnes
Davies. These two ladies, small, neat and
ever courteous, were the daughters of the
Rev Thomas Davies DD, Pastor of Bethesda
Baptist church and a noted scholar and
divine, who was mainly responsible for
founding the Welsh Baptist College at
Haverfordwest before its transfer to
Aberystwyth in 1894. Mildred and Agnes
Davies held a warm place in the respect and
affections of Haverfordwest people, running
their school with an unique mixture of
Victorian strictness and exceptional
kindness. 'Miss Agnes', as she was known,
was also active in other spheres locally and
was a much respected Justice of the Peace,
sitting regularly on the old Haverfordwest
Borough Bench.

Another part of old Haverfordwest was lost by the demolition of these houses facing down Dew Street from Sefton Square. As usual, this work was undertaken in the sacred name of road improvement and traffic flow! The van was owned by Mr Stanley Downs, a noted baker with shops on the Old Bridge, still a bakery, and Dew Street.

Swan Hotel, Swan Square, was demolished in 1968. In January 1987 the *West Wales Guardian* said: 'Haverfordians are only now beginning to realize how much of their old town and heritage has been lost to them forever through "development". One of the greatest losses is the Swan Hotel which stood for four centuries on the Swan Square. Built in 1536 it was a splendid old coach house with a busy trade, especially on mart days. It had deep cellars, spacious accommodation including a beautiful oak-panelled lounge, garages, outhouses and stabling. As late as the 1940s it employed not only the normal hotel staff but ostlers and stable boys to look after the horses and carts of the farming customers'.

The Rifleman Inn on St Thomas Green, April 1983. The last landlord was Mr Ben Moody of the famous boxing family. It was demolished in 1984 and Mr Paul Noott's pharmacy was built on the site.

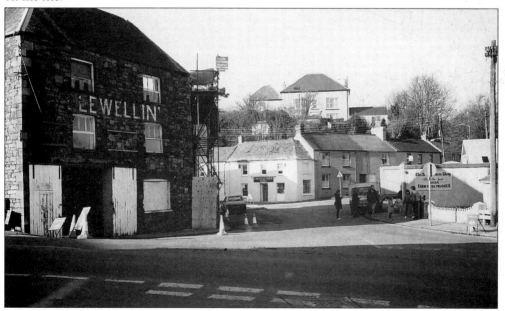

The churnworks at the bottom of Perrots Road, first established in 1789, became one of the town's principal businesses and the only one to achieve international plaudits. Founded and run for generations by the noted Llewellin family of Redhill, the churnworks produced on the premises a wide variety of dairy, agricultural and domestic goods and provided employment for many local people. But, with changing farming methods, the business closed. In 1987 the building was demolished to make way for extensive road developments.

An aerial view of the town looking south *c.* 1970. Only the railway bridge crosses the Western Cleddau downstream from the New Bridge and in the left foreground the mart ground and the Bridge Meadow are seen. The old gaol has already been converted to a county museum (moved to Scolton in the 1990s) and has had its small roof turret removed in the course of refurbishment.

The medieval castle walls overlook a scene of change in 1970 as the new Tesco store, later Iceland, is built in Picton Place, dwarfing its surroundings. To the left may be seen the old toilets which together with the adjacent weighbridge stood near Green's showrooms and beyond is the Brite Lites shop. All these latter buildings were to be swept away in the 1980s to make way for a new, dual carriageway road.

Three
Special Events

While other areas of Pembrokeshire have been subject to fluctuating fortunes over the years, Haverfordwest has remained a dignified, prosperous centre, a county town in the truest sense. 'All roads lead to Harfat' was a popular saying in former days, and it was true not only because of its geographical position right in the centre of a thriving agricultural area but because, by the enterprise of its citizens, there was always tremendous activity within its ancient town walls. All national events, such as the victories in the two world wars, the royal proclamations, processions and coronations, were celebrated with enthusiasm, and there was always a variety of local happenings which made Haverfordwest such an interesting place. Small circuses came to the town regularly, culminating in visits after the Second World War by the famous Bertram Mills and Billy Smart circuses. Haverfordwest also enjoyed exciting air shows, including that by the noted Sir Alan Cobham and his crew who set up on the Racecourse and gave flights to hundreds of Pembrokeshire people. Haverfordwest's main streets were often 'en fête' for civic events and parades by organisations like the Oddfellows, and the highly successful shopping weeks, one as long ago as 1920. For several years in the early 1930s the annual carnival attracted huge crowds from all over the county. The event, organised by Alderman L.H. Ellis (who became known locally as 'The Great Organiser') had a great reputation for the number and variety of its entries, and it raised thousands of pounds, mainly for the old County War Memorial Hospital, in those days a voluntary body.

Bill Richards

A parade of Oddfellows passing the Market Hall in Market Street, 13 August 1910.

The High Sheriff of Pembrokeshire (1902-03) Dr Henry Owen of Poyston, accompanied by the Under Sheriff, Mr W.G. Eaton-Evans; and his Chaplain, the Archdeacon of St Davids, the Venerable Williams. The occasion is the Summer Assize in May 1902. It was reported that the carriage provided for the Judge and High Sheriff was a four-horse landau driven by two postilions wearing scarlet coats, white breeches and black postilion's caps. The leading postilion – Mr William Merriman – was later to have a motor taxi in the town and in the custom of relating nicknames to occupations, was known locally as 'Taxi' Merriman. On each side are the

javelin men – the escort to the Assize Judge and High Sheriff – with two trumpeters. Originally, the javelin men were mostly yeomen tenants of the High Sheriff and were mounted 'not infrequently, as some of the escort were little used to the saddle, there would be a mishap or two, which added to the fun and merriment of the onlookers, ever ready for a laugh'. On this occasion the javelin men were the volunteer firemen of the Haverfordwest Fire Brigade. In subsequent years they were from the Haverfordwest Constabulary (see also p.35).

Two views of the Peace Day celebrations in the Castle Square on 23 July 1919, after the First World War. The day began with hymn singing by a massed choir in the Square conducted by Mr Evan Jones. Instrumentalists close to the grand piano are: Mrs Bucky Jones, High Street (pianist); Mr W.E. Dixon, Williamston (violin); and the trumpeter/bandmaster Mr J. Lewis, Bulmer House, St Thomas Green. The bearded figure in front is Mr Thompson whose son later ran the newsagency on the Bridgend Square. The little boys wearing caps to his right are Norman and Jack Holt, Prendergast, with their mother behind and their grandmother holding the baby. The celebrations included a free tea for 1,200 children in various schoolrooms, children's sports on the Bridge Meadow and a carnival in the evening.

Late nineteenth-century javelin men, outside the Milford Arms, now more correctly named the Mill Ford Arms, in Cartlett.

The javelin men at the Summer Assize, 1902. On this occasion they were the firemen of the Haverfordwest Fire Brigade, all volunteers. From left to right, front row: Messrs Davies (Barn Street), Roberts (Upper Market Street), Rogers (Barn Street); ex-Police Sergeant Irving (in charge); Messrs Simpson (Dew Street), Cook (Bridge Street). Back row: Messrs Gibbon, -?-, Morgan, Lewis (St Thomas Green), -?-, -?-, -?-. It was reported that they wore 'morning coats of a becoming design in dark-coloured cloth, scarlet waistcoats with gilt livery buttons and silk hats with cockades. The liveries which have been provided by the High Sheriff have been jointly made by Greenish and Dawkins of Market Street and Mr T. Birch, High Street. The smart turnout was very much admired by the assembled crowds and the liveries were generally voted to be very neat'.

A charabanc outing *c.* 1925 passes along Jubilee Gardens below the limekilns which in the 1930s were owned by Mr Warlow. Piles of lime can be seen on the roadside. In front of the Drill Hall are German artillery pieces captured in the First World War and later melted down for the next war. DE 1946 was a Ford truck owned by Green's Motors; DE 121, a Daimler, and DE 1007, a red Garford charabanc were both owned by J.A. Bland. Mr Percy Wilkins, 11 Dew Street owned the four-seater black Ford DE 1042. DE 1811 was a Dennis lorry owned by J.A.'s nephew, T.A. Bland. The garage of J.A. Bland, Bridgend Square, is in the background.

A mayoral procession, possibly in 1909, from St Mary's church proceeding to the Masonic Hall for a civic banquet. It is thought that the Mayor is Cllr H.J.P. (later Sir Hugh) Thomas. He is preceded by Town councillors and closely escorted by his attendants and the Haverfordwest Constabulary. On the extreme right of the picture is the Castle Hotel. Other business premises remembered in the High Street of that period are: the Gentlemen's Club; Mr Birch, tailor; Mrs Scourfield, tobacconist and confectioner; Green's, cycle shop; two doctors' surgeries; Ben Rees, ironmonger; Barclays Bank; Mrs Baggott, music shop; Tom Davies, clothier; Charlie Grey, fruiterer.

A view looking over Jubilee Gardens showing the circus coming to town in 1905. This photograph was taken before work began on the old Drill Hall which was opened with great ceremony in 1912. In Bridgend Square are the premises of J.A. Bland, carriage builder, and the copper beech tree is in its youth. The tall stone building on the left of the picture was Rowlands corn stores and later the busy agricultural stores of Archie Griffiths. In 1996 it opened as the Tourist Information Centre. The low stone building is remembered as Johnny Evans's coal yard. Between that and the corn stores was a lane to the river and at high tides the water flowed through as far as Hill Park.

Lord George Sangar's Circus approaches the Salutation Square from Jubilee Gardens in 1905. The Salutation Hotel was renamed the County Hotel in 1936. The houses in the background were demolished in the road widening scheme.

The first men in recorded history to be awarded the Honorary Freedom of the Borough of Haverfordwest were two Haverfordwest soldiers: Sergeant T.R. Thomas (St Thomas Green) and Gunner H. Morgan (Prendergast), who were awarded the Military Medal for gallantry in France during the First World War. They were both home on leave for fourteen days and are seen here on the platform. On Sunday 11 November 1917, 'after divine service at Bethesda Chapel, the Mayor and Corporation proceeded to the Castle Square where an interesting and impressive ceremony took place'.

Opening of Shopping Week by the Mayor, Cllr W.G. Rowlands, on 4 June 1920. This occasion, in the Castle Square, was reported in detail in the *Pembrokeshire Telegraph* on 9 June: 'Haverfordwest Shopping Carnival – Crowded Streets – Town En Fête – Auspicious Opening Ceremony!'

The cottage in Cuckoo Lane, Portfield Gate, on 11 September 1911 – 'blackened ruins and smouldering debris'. This event was dramatically reported in the *Haverfordwest and Milford Haven Telegraph* under the headlines: 'Terrible Double Murder – Crippled Husband's Awful Revenge – Blows Up Sleeping Wife And Child And Himself Receives Mortal Injuries – Fearful Haverfordwest Crime'. John Vaughan, a 47-year-old cripple, was obsessed by the idea that his wife had a lover and decided to kill her. Using explosives obtained from a quarry where he had previously worked, he placed the charge under the bed where his wife and eight-year-old son slept. 'By a tragic stroke the husband was unable to escape from the fired house before receiving fatal injuries. He was really overwhelmed in his own catastrophic act'. The family were buried in St Martin's cemetery. In the same cottage, a hundred years previously, another man, J. Griffiths, had also murdered his wife! There is now, however, a very respectable house on the site!

Haverfordwest Corporation Fire Brigade on the Bridge Meadow *c.* 1935. From left to right, front row: Brigade Captain Thomas Henry Davies (City Road), Brigade Lieutenant Thomas Benjamin Davies (Barn Street). Second row: Jim Nicholas, driver (Bush Row), Albert James (Hermons Hill), ? Davies (Milford Road), Arthur Jones (St Thomas Green), Clarence Phillips (Upper Market Street). Back row: W.B. Griffiths (Prendergast), Harry Phillips (Upper Market Street), Fred Howells, butcher (Dew Street), Howard Williams, waterman (Bush Row).

Withybush Airdrome was officially opened in September 1951 by Lord Ogmore, Minister for Civil Aviation. He is seen here with Colonel L.H. Higgon (Lord Lieutenant), Alderman T.R. Joseph (Chairman of Pembrokeshire County Council), Lord Ogmore, and Mayor Cllr W. Eddie Jones. The *West Wales Guardian* of 5 October reported that the ceremony was performed at the flying control tower in the presence of a representative gathering. 'Pembrokeshire Leads The Way – First County Civil Airport Opened – Three Mayors Go Flying!' After Withybush had been taken over by the County Council in May the first plane to land was piloted by a Haverfordwest man, Squadron Leader William M. Evans, an old boy of the Grammar School where he had captained both rugby and cricket teams.

The Mayor and Town councillors on the steps of the Shire Hall following the Installation Ceremony in 1950. From left to right, front row: Cllr Mrs C.I. Lloyd; the Mayor of Tenby, Cllr M. Ormond; the Mayor, Cllr R.G. Noott; the Sheriff, Cllr R. Warren; the Mayor of Pembroke, Cllr A.W. Hopkins; the Mayoress, Mrs R.G. Noott; Mrs L.T. Fisher. Middle row: Cllr Col. R.F. Foster, Cllr W.E. Jones, Ald. (Alderman) John White, Cllr L.T. Fisher, Town Clerk R. Ivor Rees, Ald. Arthur Jenkins. Back row: Cllr William Thomas, Cllr Claude Davies, Cllr Ivor Male, Rev Bowden Thomas, Cllr George Howells, the Mayor's Chaplain Rev Cope, Mr Bryn Evans (Sanitary Inspector), Ald. Walter Roberts, Cllr John Green. Cllr Noott was Mayor in 1937-38 and would be again in 1953-54.

Magistrates and officials at Haverfordwest Quarter Sessions, 1951. From left to right, seated: Mr
W. Eddie Jones, Mayor, sitting as magistrate during his term of office; Miss Maybro Phillips*;
Mrs C.I. Thomas*; Judge Rowe Harding, Chairman of Quarter Sessions; Colonel L.H. Higgon,
Lord Lieutenant; Lord Merthyr; Mrs Muriel Green*. Standing: Mr Jack Howells, Clerk; Mr H.J.
Oliver, Chief Clerk; Mr George Williams*; Mr John Thomas*; Mr Ralph Warren*; Mr George
Thomas*; Mr H.L. Underwood, Clerk of the Peace; Mr Sackville Owen (Narberth); Mr Percy
Male*; Mr Guy Noott*; Mr Howell Williams, Clerk to the Lieutenancy. * denotes magistrate
on the Haverfordwest bench. The last Quarter Sessions in Haverfordwest was held in
September 1951.

The official opening by the Mayor, Cllr R.G. Noott, of the town's first Trustee Savings Bank at
19 High Street, 17 May 1951. Well-known personalities featured include, from left to right: Mr
R.S. Lang (Headmaster, Haverfordwest Grammar School); Mr L.T. Fisher (Manager,
Cavendish Furniture); Mr Beynon (Post Master); Mr Davies (Manager, National Provincial
Bank); Cllr W.H. Thomas; Mr Scourfield (Manager, Barclays Bank); Cllr Trevor Evans; Mr D.
Hughes-Lewis; Mr J. Thomas (Accountant, Old Bridge); Mr J. Howells; Col. R.F. Foster; Ald.
R.S. Wade; Mr Tim Davies (County Librarian); Cllr R.G. Noott (in doorway), Dr D.H.
Pennant; Mrs C.I. Thomas (Western Telegraph); Mrs Harries (WVS); Cllr W. Eddie Jones;
Cllr Ivor Male; Cllr L.H. Ellis; Mr Lyn Evans (local organiser for National Savings); Mr R. Ivor
Rees (Town Clerk).

A farewell parade by 250 personnel of HMS *Goldcrest*, Brawdy, during Haverfordwest – Goldcrest Commemorative Week which marked the end of Brawdy as a Royal Naval Air Station. On 21 April 1970 the Mayor, Cllr W.S. Hayden, took the salute when the Freedom Scroll, presented by the Borough of the Town and County of Haverfordwest to HMS *Goldcrest* in 1964, was paraded through the town. The Royal Naval Air Station Brawdy was transferred from the RAF to the RN in 1946 but a government decision in 1969 that RN training for fixed-wing flying would end meant that the RN had no further use for Brawdy. From 1 April 1971 the station returned again to RAF control until 1995 when it was taken over by the Army. The photographs provide a reminder of the buildings and businesses in Castle Square and the High Street at that time.

The Town Clerk, Mr R. Ivor Rees, and bailiffs and sergeant-at-mace, accompany Alderman L.H. Ellis after he had been installed as Mayor and Admiral of the Port of Haverfordwest at the Shire Hall in May 1956. Alderman Ellis had a long and distinguished career as a Borough councillor and had been Mayor on three previous occasions in 1927-28, 1941-42, and 1942-43. He was also prominent in local sporting circles and was well known as an organiser of various events for charitable causes.

The installation of Cllr T.H. Arran as Mayor for 1970-71. On the bench in the Shire Hall, from left to right: Cllr Tom Parry, Cllr John Green, Cllr C.B. James, Cllr Glyn Rees (Sheriff), Cllr Stuart Hayden, Cllr Mrs Catherine Cole, the Mayor, Mr R. Ivor Rees (Town Clerk), Mrs Selby Arran (Mayoress), Mrs Alma Hayden, Cllr Griff Morgan, Cllr Canon R.E. Williams, and the Mayor's Chaplain. Below the Mayor are his attendants. Bailiffs: J.H. Davies (Hammond Avenue), T.H. Cole (Priory Avenue). Sergeants-at-mace: P. Hughes and J. Murphy (both of Coronation Avenue).

Led by the Mayor and Mayoress, Cllr and Mrs Donald Twigg, members of the Gild of Freemen process along St Thomas Green (with Grove Place in the background) during the Freemen's weekend in 1984. From left to right: Col. John Green (Master), Peter Higgon, Dillwyn Miles, Joan Higgon, Bill Richards, John Jones, John Walker, Dr Deri Bowen, and Malcolm Thomas. The Gild has played an active role in the town in recent years.

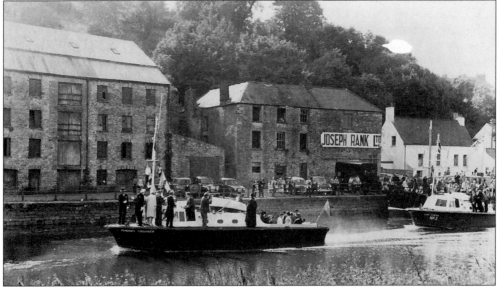

An old Haverfordwest tradition was revived after the Second World War when the Mayor of the Borough, in full regalia and accompanied by other civic dignitaries, went on an annual trip down the River Cleddau from the Old Quay to the Borough boundary near Uzmaston. The event was known as 'beating the bounds'. The old warehouses bear silent witness to Haverfordwest's former eminence as a port while the Bristol Trader inn, on the right, is evidently helping to make the trip a big social success!

Four
Sport and Pastimes

Sport has flourished in Haverfordwest for many decades, with local sides, usually sporting the traditional town colour of blue ('Come on, you Blues!'), active and successful in competition throughout both Pembrokeshire and South Wales.

The most glamorous side, since before the Second World War, has been the football club, originally Haverfordwest Athletic AFC and latterly Haverfordwest County. They have been leading members of the Welsh League, winning it on three occasions, and latterly (now under floodlights on the new Bridge Meadow, after the Safeway development), in the new League of Wales. Crowds of 1,000 were commonplace in the 1940s and '50s, with a record attendance of 6,000 for a Boxing Day derby with Pembroke Borough. Meanwhile, the club's 2nd XI was a very successful side in the Pembrokeshire League's first division throughout the 1950s and '60s.

Cricket has been played on the Racecourse since the Enclosure Act of 1838 and Haverfordwest Cricket Club is certainly among the very first in Wales. After the Second World War there were two flourishing sides playing on the Lower Racecourse: Haverfordwest and the Thomarians. In the mid-1960s Haverfordwest and 'the Toms' merged and the town side went on from strength to strength, opening their new clubhouse on the Upper Racecourse in 1977.

Haverfordwest has also always had a strong local rugby side, playing in turn on the Rifleman Field, on the Fishguard Road ground, and latterly, on their new ground on the Pembroke Road. Highlight of the season for many years was the Boxing Day derby against old rivals Llangwm for the Bishop Cup. There was also a succession of powerful rugby teams from the Grammar School.

Many other sports have flourished: golf, hockey, bowls and tennis among them. The latter two have been played since 1935 at the delightful ground at the Parade which has for many years been host to the county lawn tennis finals.

Robert Nisbet

A nostalgic scene, especially for football fans –the Bridge Meadow before the big developments, the occasion being a cup match early in 1994 between Carew and Saundersfoot Sports.

Haverfordwest Grammar School rugby side pictured at Haverfordwest station in 1958, on their way to the Roehampton Sevens in Richmond. As the school was a member of the Headmasters' Conference, the team regularly competed at the top level of public school rugby. From left to right: Mr Wally Ladd, David Roberts, Alan Rees, Bert Jones, Clive Morgan, Michael Fry, Brian John, Mr R.S. Lang (Headmaster), David Banner, Maurice Palmer, Alan John, Mr Meurig Hughes (coach), Alderman Leslie Ellis.

Haverfordwest Grammar School rugby 1st XV in 1956, one of the most successful in a line of powerful teams produced by the school. They regularly played and beat many leading schools, public schools included. The scrum-half and captain, Maurice Palmer, seen here wearing his Welsh shirt, played that year for Welsh Schools, and later won an Oxford blue. From left to right, front row: J. Williams, Bert Jones, Alan Havard, Hugh Phillips. Middle row: Mr Wally Ladd, David Roberts, Brian Mair, Roy Harries, Maurice Palmer (captain), Alan John, Malcolm Edgar, B.J. Roberts. Back row: David Cole, Brian John, John Roberts, Michael Fry, Lyndon Morgan, Michael Edwards, David Ward, Roger Thomas, Roger Harper, J.N.O. Harries.

Haverfordwest Athletic AFC 1st XI pictured in the 1958-59 season shortly after they had won the Welsh League first division title for the first time. The young mascot is Tommy Lewis from Merlins Bridge while the trainer is the redoubtable Billy Williams, a noted character whose sponge and water were poised ready for any injury! This was the nucleus of the side which had pulled off a spectacular success in the previous season by holding Cardiff City's 1st XI to a 2-2 draw in a Welsh Cup tie on the Bridge Meadow. From left to right, front row: Ralph Baker, Alan Williams, John Foxton (captain, with Tommy Lewis, mascot), Ray Chennard, John Jones, Billy Williams (trainer). Back row: Gwilym Cain, Johnny Williams, Stan Richards, John Thomas, Cliff Pawlett, Islwyn Griffiths.

Haverfordwest Cricket Club 1st XI pictured around 1970, at the start of two of the most successful decades in the club's history. Many of the young players pictured here formed the nucleus of the side for nearly twenty years and several (notably Stuart Williams, Tony Myles and Micky Field) were leading players with the club into the 1990s. From left to right, front row: Stephen Price, Tony Myles, Stuart Williams (captain), Peter Bricknell, Hugh Phillips. Back row: Donald Twigg, Peter Lewis, Mickey Field, David Isaac, Bob Berry, John Lewis.

Haverfordwest Rugby Club 1st XV with some of the club officials at the end of the 1950-51 season. The team played then on the Rifleman Field and is pictured here behind Nicholas' Garage. From left to right, front row: M. Bishop, S. Lucas, L. Watts, P. Lewis, G. Dickenson. Middle row: W.W. Ladd, R. Ovens, W. Rees (captain), R. Phillips, H. Scale (vice-captain), J.H. Bishop (who presented the Bishop Cup in 1947-48). Back row: K. Howel, E.C.A. Phillips, H.S. James, M. Thomas, M. Beasley, R. Wood, D. Pritchard, P. Phillips, J. Griffiths, N. Nicholson, G. Davies, J.B. Ebsworth, O. Griffiths.

Haverfordwest Athletic AFC 2nd XI, for some years one of the high-flying sides in the Pembrokeshire League, pictured here before a cup final against Milford United in 1961. They lost 2-1, but in the same season won the League championship. From left to right, front row: Mostyn Rowlands, Billy Thomas. Seated: John Evans, Cecil Williams, Mervyn Thomas, Royden Davies, Councillor Harold Arran (Chairman of the Pembrokeshire Football Association). Back row: Cliff Lewis, Harry Burke, Donald Twigg, Cliff Pawlett, John Tilley, Colin Ellis, Hugh James, Hugh Phillips, Henry Walters.

Haverfordwest ATC 948 Squadron football team were for several years by far the best ATC side in Wales. They are shown here in 1960, before a cup final on the Bridge Meadow, in which they beat Swansea ATC 3-0. In that season, seven of the team represented Wales and one of them, David Tozer, played for Great Britain ATC. From left to right, front row: John Watts, Vernon Hodgens, Ernie Nicholas, Gerald Williams, David Tozer. Back row: Revd R.E. Williams, Mr Evans, Wynford Morse, Hugh Williams, David Vaughan, Ronnie John, Paul Gibby, Carl Williams; the officer commanding, Flt. Lt. Eddie Steadman, and a visitor from Swansea ATC.

The traditional Boxing Day meet in the Castle Square. The Pembrokeshire Foxhounds in 1959, led by the joint master, Mr Tom Jones (right) with kennel huntsman, Mr Sidney Lewis, move off from the Castle Square. The local paper reported that there were over a thousand spectators and over eighty riders followed hounds. Hylton John, outfitters, now occupies the building of Boots the chemist and Granada Television is on the site of the demolished Pearl Assurance offices, Victoria House.

Haverfordwest Golf Club at Arnolds Down was officially opened on Thursday 12 July 1934 by Sir Henry Philipps, Picton Castle. It was a nine-hole course and the clubhouse was a former army hut purchased at a knockdown price from a site in the south of the county – a far cry from today's luxury surroundings and 18-hole course with ever burgeoning membership. Haverfordwest Golf Club was established in 1904 at the Racecourse where it operated successfully for thirty years before other demands on the open space there caused the club to seek a move.

Presentation of trophies at Haverfordwest Golf Club annual meeting in December 1960. In front the club captain, Bill Richards, presents the captain's prize to Ronald Noott. In the second row, from left to right: Roderick Thomas, Bill Thomas, Alex Jones (secretary), Billy John. Behind: Mel Carr, Hector Hammond (president), Ted Davies (vice-captain), Stan Levis and John Rees (treasurer). Earlier in the season Bill Richards had said facetiously that the captain's prize that year would be a Rolls Royce. He kept his promise by presenting Ronald Noott with a miniature of the famous motor car in addition to an inscribed tankard.

Leading tennis players and supporters of the Haverfordwest Lawn Tennis club on The Parade courts during a Festival of Britain tournament, 23 June 1951. From left to right, seated: J.H.A. Macken, Sir Tom Ince Webb-Bowen, Miss Iris Howells, Miss Pam Morris, Mrs Bevans, Lady Webb-Bowen. Standing: W. Bevans, Joan Tucker, C. Richards, Lily Thomas, N. Davies, Miss A. Webb-Bowen, C. Evans, Miss A. Voyle, R. Griffiths, Miss I. Griffiths, Miss P. Cleevely, M. Roberts, and P. Lewis.

Several Haverfordwest ladies played for Neyland Ladies/St Trinians hockey team in the Neyland 'It's A Knock-Out' competition on the rugby ground c. 1970. Pictured are, front row: Pauline Blight (Haverfordwest), Janet Summons (Johnston), Gill Raymond, Pat Davies, Margaret Harries (all Haverfordwest). Second row: Janet Tapley (Neyland), Jeanette Davies, Shirley Jones (both Johnston), Elizabeth Davies (Milford), Rosemary Bray (Neyland).

Haverfordwest Youth Centre athletic team (Rosemary Lane Youth Club), 1951. This was the first youth club formed in the county and in 1951 they won the Championship Shield for the third time at the County Youth Sports. From left to right, front row: Edwina Bowen, Doris Newman, Dilys Watts, Betty Potter. Kneeling: Brian Harries, John Davies, Leslie James, Derek Edgar. Standing: Mr J. Watts (trainer), Derek Rees, Peter Phillips, David Lewis, Gordon Lewis, Cedric Davies, Tony Steele-Morgan, Billy Lewis, Gerald Laugharne, Mr D.C. Evans (youth leader). In 1946 Pembrokeshire County Council was in the vanguard of local authorities providing facilities for young people when the former stable block in Rosemary Lane (see page 27) was converted for use as a youth centre.

An evocative photograph of Mr Willie Davies, Uzmaston Farm, working with his sheepdogs. A breeder of dogs since boyhood days, Mr Davies became a registered breeder of Scotch Border Collies in the early 1950s since when his dogs have won many prizes including the South Wales Open Novice Championship. An official show judge for over fifty years, he served as Welsh National President of the International Sheep Dog Society from 1982 to 1985.

Captain John Tucker Edwardes (1809-1891) was the real founder of the Sealyham breed. The terrier was named after the residence of the breeder. He was anxious to breed a short-legged, smart, workman-like terrier which would, above all, be courageous. As a show dog the Sealyham terrier was first exhibited in Haverfordwest, the town of its origin, on 3 October 1903 and was recognised by the Kennel Club in 1910.

Mr Roy Vaughan with his home-bred Sealyham terrier bitch – Champion Rosvon Rita. She won three challenge certificates in 1964, the most prestigious being at the National Terrier Club Championship show. With them is the Sealyham Terrier Club's beautiful silver Perpetual Challenge Cup valued at 100 guineas in 1908. In recent years, however, the number of Sealyhams kept in Pembrokeshire has fallen off drastically and sadly the Sealyham Terrier Club and its prized trophies are no longer based in Haverfordwest.

Two distinctive breeds – the Pembrokeshire Corgi and the Sealyham Terrier – featured regularly in the town's dog shows from the early years of the century. The local officials of both the Welsh Corgi Club and Sealyham Terrier Club were often members of the dog show committees. Recognised in this group are: one-time President, Capt Jack Howell, and committee members Fred Munt, Ocky White, Dickie Howell, Sid Bowler with his daughter Thora, and G. Checkland-Williams.

Mr Sidney Bowler and his daughter, Mrs Thora Jenkins, in 1942 with some of their prize-winning Pembrokeshire corgis.

Five
Business and Commerce

The commercial history of Haverfordwest dates back many hundreds of years. It was a flourishing port and trading centre when Cardiff was still a village! During the early part of the nineteenth century it was the chief port on the western coast of Wales and a thriving trade was carried out with London, Bristol, Dublin, France, Spain and Portugal.

It was the extension of the railway line to the town in 1853 which sounded the death knell of Haverfordwest as a tidal port but which, at the same time, enhanced its reputation as the principal town of the county. Because of its central position in Pembrokeshire it continued to expand as the 'octopus' mouth of the county through which agricultural products and manufactured goods were distributed.

Many of the great town houses of the landed gentry were built at the top end of the town in Hill Street and Goat Street, to be followed in later years by the county offices, hospital, library, hiring fairs and the Market Hall. Thus it was that Market Street was a very important shopping area. Unfortunately perhaps, trade, like water, tends to run downhill, and slowly there was a movement of businesses from Market Street down to High Street. The relocation of the post office from a dominant position in High Street to Quay Street in 1936 and the arrival of Woolworths and the multiple national grocers foreshadowed today's development of Bridge Street, Quay Street and the riverside area.

Haverfordwest's topography of steep hills and narrow streets and the public desire for one-stop 'leisure' shopping saw a development towards out of town shopping with Vincent Davies & Son, a very old established family business converting from a wholesale grocers to a large centre at Withybush whilst Tesco moved from an in-town position in Picton Place to a large supermarket covering several acres on the outskirts at Portfield.

Fortunately, the business character of the town though changed, still has well-established family enterprises that have been handed down through three, four, or even five generations: J. & G. Bland (Motors) Ltd, County Clothes, Green's Motors Ltd, Ocky White Ltd, Roch James, and Bisley H. Munt, jewellers, which was established over two hundred years ago. Haverfordwest, however, is still in danger of becoming a town without a heart as private traders shrink in numbers to be replaced by multiples requiring out-of-town sites with adequate parking.

John White

A cattle fair at St Thomas Green in the early twentieth century. Even in 1936 the Borough Council were discussing the removal of the martground to a site nearer the railway station!

Busy trading at the Swan Square martground in November 1953. On mart days mid-Pembrokeshire farmers came into town in droves and gave a great fillip to local trade.

Gwyneth and Stanley Howells of Prendergast delivering milk in front of Holloways garage, Salutation Square, after the blizzard in 1947.

Rees Howells' shop opposite Cartlett Stores.

This rather unprepossessing thoroughfare, photographed in 1982, was known to most Haverfordians as 'Behind the Track'. It ran from Cartlett Road behind the former Green's Motors building and on to the Old Bridge area. The motor repair garage on the left was run for many years by Mr Alfred Phillips and his son Glyn.

The West Cambrian power station in Cartlett was a feature among the buildings in the lower part of Haverfordwest for many years until its demolition in 1987. Residents remember the noise and vibration from the generators causing ornaments and fittings to rattle in houses many hundreds of yards away. Green's Motors now occupy the site.

The new Morris Minor, at Bland's Garage, Bridgend Square, March 1956.

Staff of J. & G. Bland (Motors) Ltd in 1968, taken on the retirement of Mr Harold Davies, City Road, who had completed sixty years with the firm broken only by service during the First World War. From left to right, front row: Ernie Williams, Grant Davies, Alan Bland, Gordon Bland, Harold Davies, Ronald Mills, Tim Hardaker. Middle row: Elizabeth Parry, Duncan Thomas, Clifford Bevan, Harry Hall, Marcel Absalom, Richard Wade, Donald Hooper, Ann Riley. Back row: Philip Bevan, Ray Lewis, Alun Hughes, Billy Owen, Dawson Webb, Graham Watts, Barry Brock.

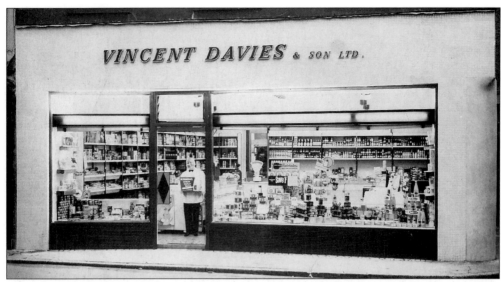

One of the well-known local businesses, the grocery store of Vincent Davies & Son, in 1959. The firm started trading from No 1 Bridge Street in 1906. They moved to No 42 (later occupied by John Bull stores) in 1915, later moving to No 44, and for a time occupying the premises at both 42 and 44. In 1966 they moved to their present superstore on the Fishguard Road but later re-opened the Bridge Street store which now trades as the 'Moon and Sixpence'. Four generations have traded in the town, Mr Vincent Davies being succeeded in the business by his son, Mr Ralph Vincent-Davies, and then by Ralph's two sons, Mr John and Dr Stephen Vincent-Davies. Stephen's daughter Lindsey is currently managing the 'Moon and Sixpence'.

The Vincent Davies family c. 1936. From left to right, front row: Mr Vincent Davies, Owain, Mrs Maud Davies. Back row: Mabel, Evangeline, Alice, Ralph, Ceinwen, Gwladys.

Leslie Brinley Pugh (1884-1944) had a highly respected hairdressing and tobacconist business at 11 Bridge Street, next to The Hole in the Wall, for nearly forty years, from c. 1904 until his sudden death in 1944. Among his older customers were many who had continued to patronise him throughout his time in business. In 1922, Hugh Devonald, aged fifteen, was apprenticed to Mr Pugh then at a weekly wage of 4/- and remained until called up for the RAF in 1941. He, too, became recognised as a skilled craftsman who, like L.B. Pugh, took great pride in his work. By 1939 the weekly wage had risen to £2 but the hours were long – 8.30 to 6pm daily – and on Saturdays when the 'country came to town' the shop stayed open until 10pm!

A. Scale, Children's Outfitters, 25 Bridge Street. Opened by Arthur and Alice Scale in 1922, it enjoyed an enviable reputation as a quality children's outfitters until their daughter Joan retired in 1988. Both Arthur and Alice were from local farming stock; Arthur was born at Annykell and Alice, one of fourteen children, next door at Bolton Hill. Prior to service in the First World War, Arthur learned the outfitter's trade in London where he was apprenticed with Harrods. Alice trained as a nurse at the old infirmary on St Thomas Green before also moving to London. It was as well that Arthur, who had also set himself up as a turf accountant, had some adventurous county clients and a stable of good point-to-point horses for Alice's takings for the first week amounted to only 7/6. As both businesses prospered Arthur could indulge his favourite sport of fishing the Cleddau from Cutty Bridge down to his own back door at Skinners Lane.

Bridge End Square Shop in 1985. This unusual shop was a feature of the town until its demolition for the 1987 road scheme. It was built *c.* 1919 as a lock-up shop and was first occupied by Mr Thompson as a retail newsagents shop. When Mr Thompson moved next door (below) it was used as a greengrocers and later for boot and shoe repairs. In 1932 Mr Albert Devereux opened it as a tailor's shop, expanding the following year with a chicken shed bought from Llewellin's Churnworks for £12. 10s. During the Second World War he was unable to obtain cord and cloth and became a retail clothier selling both new and second-hand clothing. In 1952 Mr Devereux retired and was succeeded by his son Norman.

Mr W.H. ('Bill') Thompson's stationery shop, known locally as 'Thompson's'. The shop and the rifle range alongside it were also demolished with the new road scheme at Bridgend Square in 1987.

The County Theatre, which for fifty years was one of Haverfordwest's most popular places of entertainment. With the introduction of 'the talkies' in the late 1920s, the West of England Cinema Company acquired Lewis the furnishers and within months the old premises had gone and a large modern building was rising in its place at a reputed cost of £28,000, an enormous sum in those days. Aesthetically it was no masterpiece, but Haverfordwest loved it and from its official opening in February 1935, it served the town and district not only as a cinema but as a centre for various entertainments. It became one of the town's great assets and there was genuine regret when, with the decline of the cinema, the building was sold and subsequently demolished. The cinema accommodated 1,200 people and included a full theatre stage, dressing rooms, a large café and a sprung dance floor. Two familiar residents are seen here chatting in front of the old theatre: Mr Jock Gallagher (left), well-known painter and decorator, and right, Mr W.H. Jones JP, who for many years was Chief Executive of the Pembrokeshire War Agricultural Committee.

A typical Bridge Street business of former days – Harries the chemist. There was a chemist's shop on this site for generations, run by Mr J.L. Jenkins for many years and then by Mr Basil Jones and his wife, Myfanwy (*née* Bleddyn), for a very long period until it was taken over by Mr Joseph Harries and his brother after the Second World War. It was long regarded as one of the town's most successful businesses.

Initially operating as pianoforte dealers and tuners from premises in Cartlett, the business moved to Victoria Place. While always known principally as a music shop, McKenzie's changed with the times and also sold a variety of small goods including the famous Dinky toys which became so popular during and after the Second World War. For years the business was run by William McKenzie who became one of the town's noted characters. He was extrovert, outspoken and witty which often caused consternation among fellow townspeople. He served on the Borough Council for several years, where, due to his forthright manner, he was often the centre of controversy. After William McKenzie's days the shop was run for many years by his son and daughter, Leslie and Ethel.

McKenzie's shop-front in Victoria Place c. 1960, formerly one of Haverfordwest's most popular businesses.

In 1921 Octavius John White, a dynamic 34-year-old, opened his first shop in Haverfordwest here at 13 High Street, then immediately opposite the post office and next to W.H. Smith. Trading on three floors, it was an emporium catering for the needs of the whole family and renowned for its well known motto – S. P. Q. R. – small profit, quick return. In 1929 it moved to its present spacious site in Bridge Street where it continues to develop as 'Pembrokeshire's Leading Store'.

This family business has been prominent in Haverfordwest since its opening by Tom Davies at 24 High Street in 1901. His great-grandson joined the business in 1996 as the fourth generation in the firm. Following the founder's death in 1925, he was succeeded by his son Tom Rhys Davies who, with the help of his family, established it as one of the quality shops of the town. Now under the direction of their son Anthony, the business has extended its range of quality merchandise to include kitchen-ware, glass and ceramics.

It was said that at Herbert's ironmonger's shop in Market Street one could buy anything from a safety pin to a steamroller! A slight exaggeration, of course, but there is no doubt that the Herbert brothers, Lewis and Wilfred, did maintain an extraordinary stock of goods to supplement the ironmongery business on which the business was founded early in the century. The two brothers were highly individualistic in their attitudes, even to their customers, but were recognised as good businessmen and their shop was always well patronised, especially by local country folk.

Left: Truly a landmark property in the town's High Street, its projecting clock appearing in innumerable old photographs. The clock was erected c. 1880 to be followed a few years later by a new shop-front which today continues to make the frontage so significant and distinctive. The original business was established in 1796, the Munt connection dating from c. 1872 when Bisley Henry Munt came to Haverfordwest to assist in the business, becoming proprietor in 1880. Still very much a family concern, Mr John Munt, the fourth generation, took over the business following his father's death in 1993 and with three sons, it seems likely that 'Munt's the Jewellers' will remain in the town well into the next century.

Parry's Garage, Dew Street, c. 1956. In 1949 the garage consisted of just two small rooms. In 1951, however, Mr James Parry, a motor engineer who had lived in Haverfordwest for twenty years, extended the business, County Motors, to 'one of the largest and most pleasantly designed showrooms in the area'. He held four agencies – Sunbeam Talbot, Humber, Hillman and Commer. There were four petrol pumps on the forecourt. The Rolls-Royce – BUC 1 – was well-known in the district when it belonged to Haverfordwest dentist, David Tudor-Williams. It was built in 1934 on a Rolls-Royce chassis 20/25 with a Sedanka-de-Ville body by Parkward and was rebuilt c. 1948 in the style of a post-war Rolls. It left Pembrokeshire c. 1970 and now 'lives' with a Rolls-Royce enthusiast in Godalming, Surrey.

Haverfordwest's old slaughterhouse at the top of Milford Road. A robust example of Victorian commercial building dating from c. 1880, and a hub of activity in former days. With the changing times the slaughterhouse eventually outlived its usefulness, Its architectural qualities did not save it from demolition and in 1987 it was replaced by a housing complex, Hanover Court.

The wholesale and retail grocery business of William John & Son, 2 Quay Street *c*. 1920. A grocery business was established here in 1823. William John (1836-1927) became an assistant in 1857 and later foreman, eventually becoming a partner in 1864 before taking over the business in 1885. He was one of the most notable figures in Pembrokeshire and a magistrate on the Haverfordwest bench. In 1898 his eldest son, also William (1870-1962), became a partner in the business and, like his father, a local magistrate. Heavy death duties following the death of Mr John in 1927 and changes in the grocery retail trade caused the business to close *c*. 1935 and the premises remained empty until it was requisitioned in 1939 for use by the Local Defence Volunteers (later the Home Guard) and Air Raid Wardens. It is now owned by Howells (West Wales Jewellers) Ltd.

Edward Nicholas, pictured *c*. 1925, in front of his blacksmith's shop on St Thomas Green, next to the present Londis shop.

Six

Schools

Education, always a priority in Wales, seems to have been no less so in Haverfordwest. Before education became the responsibility of the state in 1870 and primary education became compulsory and free of expense in 1880 there were many benefactors in the area.

The exact origins of Haverfordwest Grammar School are unclear but it was probably associated with the Augustinian Priory as early as the twelfth century. It was certainly in existence in 1488 when the then Bishop of St Davids appointed a master 'to inform unlearned youths in grammar and other liberal sciences'. In 1684 Mrs Mary Tasker of Rudbaxton bequeathed her farm at East Dudwell to be used as a charity school for 'poor children of both sexes between the ages of nine and thirteen years'. In 1884 this became Taskers High School for Girls after occupying several sites in the town during the intervening period. From 1699, Sir John Philipps of Picton Castle under the auspices of the Society for Promoting Christian Knowledge was another philanthropist who helped establish many charity schools for primary education in the town.

In the late nineteenth century, local people set up small private schools, often women in their own homes (dame schools), sometimes churchmen and many others. Most of these had little or no training and standards were generally poor. However, schooling gradually became available to more children and flourished under state and church into the twentieth century.

Old school photographs must be amongst the most nostalgic and evocative of all. The clothes, appearance and attitude of the groups are a microcosm of social history and shows the young people, with their mentors, on the threshold of life.

Joy Roach

Little infants at Prendergast school c. 1920. The pleasing buildings with their belltowers and tall chimneys are in stark contrast to the boxed appearance of so many of our schools today.

The staff and pupils of Hill House College in 1923. They include relatives of many families well known in the locality, and children from Milford, Pembroke and the surrounding areas were boarders. From left to right, kneeling in the front row: Billy Munt, Ellerslie Bland, Norah Llewellin, Marjorie McKeown, Phyllis Bland, Vida Jones, Roma Kendall, Iris Belton, Jackie Crabb, David Llewellin, David Masterman. Seated: Miss Martin (who lived in Prendergast and is remembered as a kind and efficient teacher), Miss Agnes Davies, Miss Gertrude Davies, Thora Bowler, Molly Crabb, Eva Backhouse (Milford), -?-, -?-, Blodwen ?, ? Rees, Betty Joyce, Mary Bland, Ina Reynolds, Doris Crabb, Elsie George (Camrose), Nancy Roach (Pembroke), Miss Mildred Davies, Miss Fowlds (Aberystwyth). Third row: Miss Clark, -?-, -?-, Winnie Llewellyn, Mary George, -?-, -?-, Connie Thomas, three cousins (names uncertain), -?-, Penelope Harries, Molly Evans, Molly Phipps, ? Lewis, -?-, -?-. Back row: Mavis Reynish, Peggy Richards (Pearson), -?-, -?-, -?-, Kitty Masterman, Minnie Phillips, Nesta Roach, Molly Llewellyn, ? Davies, Gertrude Mathias (Hoaten), -?-, Iris Hughes (Milford), Ivy Ramster (Milford).

The staff of St Martin's School, 1934-35, then occupying the Tabernacle chapel schoolroom. From left to right, seated: Margaret Charles, Emily Davies, Emma Howell (Headmistress), Nelly Bill. Standing: Bessie Pettit, Miss Lena John, Ruth Max.

Pupils of Rhos School, early 1960s. From left to right, seated: Carol Nobes, Elizabeth Kelly, Karen Ekkes, Elizabeth Bowen, Stephen Griffiths, Allan Nobes, Simon Elworthy, John Curran, Marion Davies, Christine Morgan, Gillian Collins, Betty Davies. Second row: David Bennett, Phillip Jenkins, Gareth Griffiths, Janet Morgan, Jackie Ekkes, Daphne Edwards, Moira Morgan, Jane Owen, David Edwards, Allan Collins, Robert Bowen. Back row: Miss Ethel Evans, Mark Curran, Ken Smith, Robert Griffiths, Calvin Morgan, Roger Jenkins, Graham Owen, Peter Owen, John Rees, Mr Wilfred Morgan (Head teacher). The school, on the Slebech estate, opened in 1866. By the early 1980s Dyfed Education Committee wished to close the school in a reorganisation programme. While the Church in Wales was sympathetic to the idea, there was strong local opposition. However, the school did finally close in 1985 and is now a private residence.

A class at Fenton Infants School c. 1959. The teachers are Miss F.A. Smith (headmistress) (right), and Miss Betty Crockett who became headmistress in 1961. These two ladies between them totalled 48 years of service as head teachers at the school. The children are, from left to right, front row: Helen Davies, Sue James, -?-, Rosalyn James, Elizabeth Rodney, Margaret Shearne, Janet Davies, Jill Evans, Elizabeth Swales. Second row: Ian Mathias, Richard John, Paul Phillips, Keith Pridmore, Peter Nicholls, Peter John, David Owen, Gary Evans. Back row: Geoffrey Higgs, Michael Sanderson, -?-, Keith Turner, Nigel Whittow, John Roberts, David Miller, Nigel Voyle, Timothy Green.

The teaching staff of Prendergast Girls' School in 1948. From left to right, seated: Mrs Alice Morgan, Miss Lavinia Lawrence (Headmistress), Miss Phyllis Hancock. Standing: Miss Gina Hughes, Miss Beryl Hosker, Miss Chris Wheeler, Miss Betty Protheroe.

The staff of Fenton Infants School c. 1959. From left to right, seated: Peggy Bushell, Miss F.A. Smith (Head teacher), Olive Evans. Standing: Clara Parry, Dilys Parry, Glenda Vaughan, Betty Crockett.

The staff of Mount Airey School *c.* 1970. From left to right, seated: Barbara Tubb, Eirwen Golding, Margaret Allen, Enid Williams (Head teacher). Standing: Enid Davies and Bronnie Griffiths.

A class at Mount Airey Infants School in 1972 with their teacher Mrs Barbara Tubb. From left to right, seated: Tanya Sinnet, Helen Morgan, Linda Hastings, Gillian Vaughan, Ann White, Gaynor Toop, Elizabeth Roch James. Second row: Timothy Payne, -?-, Wendy Morris, Kim James, Lucy Ann Hay, Siân Hockley, Theresa Watts, ? Lewis, Simon Turley. Back row: Paul Thomas, Mark Lowe, D. Laugharne, -?-, Jonathan ?.

Taskers School Choir with their conductor and music mistress, Miss Margaret Bushell, in the Pontcanna studio, Cardiff, after their television appearance in February 1966. From left to right, front row: Fiona Pealing, Carol Davies, Jane Dole, Vanessa John, Hilary Beynon. Second row: Shirley Owen, Elizabeth Swales, Margaret Shearn, Christine Hemmings, Sara Evans, Virginia Sturgess, Elizabeth Parry. Third row: Ann Henton, Christine Kelly, Siân Davies, Siegrid Heldt, Mandy Rudder, Gillian Thomas. Back row: Elizabeth James, Heather Beynon, Marilyn Shearn, Moira Scourfield, Siân Miles, Ann Thomas, Ann Havard.

Taskers High School for Girls orchestra after winning first prize in the senior school orchestral competition in the National Eisteddfod at Bridgend in 1948. The test piece was Mozart's *Eine Kleine Nachtmusik*. From left to right, seated: Linda Robbins, Auriel Bryant, Ruth Ivemey (conductor), Mrs C.E. Thomas (trainer and accompanist), Betty Williams (leader), Mrs M. Hughes Phillips (Welsh teacher), Shirley Robbins, Mair Ivemey. Standing; Terry Potter, Rose Berry. June Howells, June Griffiths, Jill Rowlands, Doris Phillips, Vivienne Lawrence, Margaret Davies, Nan Peters, Sheila Owen.

Opening the new Taskers school in Portfield, 1962. Mr Walter Barrett, County Architect, hands the souvenir key to Mrs Rosemary Donnelly, the wife of Desmond Donnelly MP. From left to right: Canon Bowden Thomas; Cllr John Daniels; Ald. Evan Anthony, Chairman of the Pembrokeshire Education Authority; Cllr Sydney Rees; Mr Wynford Davies, Director of Education; Ald. Ralph Warren JP, Chairman of the School Governors; Mr Barrett; Miss A.G. Rees, Headmistress; Mrs Donnelly.

The presentation by Mrs Valerie Payne on behalf of the Taskers Old Girls Association to Miss A.G. Rees MSc, Headmistress of Taskers Grammar School for Girls, on the occasion of her retirement in 1966. She had been headmistress of the school since 1948 and during that time had initiated many changes in the curriculum as well as being responsible for the school's relocation from Tower Hill to Portfield in 1962. From left to right, standing: Mrs Audrey Thomas, Mrs Linda Richards, Miss Ida Griffiths, Mrs Gertrude Thomas, Miss A.G. Rees, Miss June Evans, Mrs Valerie Payne, Miss Margaret Bushell, Mrs Janet Llewellyn, Mrs Margaret Munt.

Haverfordwest Grammar School orchestra, 1978. From left to right, front row: David Evans, Peter Horton, David Gregory, ? Collins, Mr F.F. Nicholls, Dr J.S. Miller, Mr W.G. Thomas (Headmaster), Mr J. Swales MBE (Director), Mr C.H. Willcock, Mr M. Watts, Paul Willcock, Webb, Dean Morris. Middle row: Ian Thomas, Richard Parry, -?-, Philip Nicolle, Danny McBrearty, Frank Trew, Stephen Thomas, Wyn Thomas, Ian Wright. Back row: Martin Beddows, ? Langley, ? Jones, Nigel Jones, Dominic Murcott, Damien Golden, David Devonald, Christian, Stephen Phelps, Toby Murcott, Nicholas Cale.

The original school orchestra had been formed and trained by Mr Griffin Bishop, organist of St Mary's church. Following the appointment of Mr W.G. Thomas as Headmaster in 1958, Mr Joffre Swales MBE was invited to reform the orchestra to include woodwind, brass and percussion sections. As well as performing at the annual speech days, concerts were given in the old Market Hall in Market Street. At one memorable concert, Maurice Sheppard, a talented young pupil, played his own piano concerto and on another occasion a tone poem he had composed entitled Newgale.

Lined up across Dew Street for the start of the Haverfordwest Grammar School annual cross-country run, 29 March 1928 – at 2.30 pm! 'Following three days rain the 'going' was particularly heavy and the course was completed in fifty-three minutes by Leslie Williams (Johnston), with F. Pugh Davies (Haverfordwest) only two seconds behind'. Bob Saies and Trevor Jones, both Haverfordwest, were third and fourth. Included, from left to right are: Mr R.T.P. Williams, Chairman of the Governors and starter; Mr R.S. Lang, Headmaster 1927-1958; Mr Johnson, house master; Frank Pugh Davies, Leslie Williams, Idris Davies, Harold Martin, Morris Laycock, Ivor Warlow, Billy McClean, Jack Shepherd, ? James, Peter Sage, Arnold Thomas, Trevor Jones, Noel Rees, Bob Saies, Robin Jones, ? Prickett, Morgan Griffiths, Cyril Rea, Wilfred Harries, J.F. Jeffreys, A.G. Bishop, Jack Thomas, Alan Watts, John Jones, Gwilym Williams.

Haverfordwest Grammar School gymnastic team, 1926, in the Drill Hall. From left to right, front row: Malcolm Roberts (Neyland), Nigel Bishop (Haverfordwest, son of the organist of St Mary's church), seated; C.T. Davies (Haverfordwest), Ron Batte (Neyland), Mr Aspinall, Stanley Green and A.G. Bishop (both Haverfordwest). Back row: Hughie Holt (Haverfordwest), Trevor Evans (Haverfordwest), Jones, H.D. Burry (Haverfordwest), Reggie Saunders (Neyland), Dave Edmonds (Haverfordwest).

This ink drawing by B.J. Allen appeared in the final edition of *The Haverfordian*, 1962/63, published from the premises in Dew Street before the school moved to the new site in Scarrowscant. The fives court will be well remembered for informal ball games and 'where boys went to settle their differences'. Brian Allen went on to take a diploma in Art and Design at Newport College of Art and a postgraduate degree course at Birmingham College of Art before returning to join the staff at Newport. He is presently Head of the Art department at an independent school in North Wales.

The staff of Haverfordwest Grammar School during the summer term, 1959. From left to right, seated: G.T. Williams, Mrs O.W. Robinson (Secretary), H.H. Betty (Head of Classics), W. Mangan (Deputy Head and Head of French), W.G. Thomas* (Headmaster), C.M. Round (Head of Maths), L.C. Thomas*, W.W. Ladd*, R. Redd (Head of Chemistry). Standing: M.J. Bristow (Head of Geography), T.G. Thomas (Head of PE), F.F. Nicholls* (Head of English), W.R. Jenkins, C.H. Wilcock* (Head of History), P.J. Brown (Head of Biology), L.N. Williams (Head of Music), R.A. Lowe (Head of Art), D.G. Roch*, R.F. Ray*, E.H. Haines* (Head of Physics). Those marked * were still at the school when it closed in 1978.

The fourth-year class at the County Secondary Modern School in 1960. From left to right, front row: Anita Lloyd (Neyland), Valmai Walters (Rosemarket), Pam Evans (Clarbeston Road), Angela Williams, Margaret Evans (both Haverfordwest), Second row: Sandra Warlow (Neyland), Mary Rogers (Haverfordwest), Winifred Phillips (Hook), Monica Davies (Burton), Kathleen O'Neil (Haverfordwest), Anne Talbot (Neyland), Pamela Clarke (Haverfordwest), Megan Adams (Crundale), Celia Frith (whose father was stationed at Brawdy). Back row: Meyrick Williams (Clarbeston Road), Nadine Palmer, Pat Dillon, Mr Mervyn Williams (form master of 4S). Betty Lewis, James Sweeney, Gerald Rees, Jennifer Charles, George Blockwell (all Haverfordwest).

The staff of Haverfordwest County Secondary Modern School in its first year – 1952. From left to right, front row: Gina Hughes, Dorothy Thomas, Lucille Daniels, Roger Morgan (Senior Master), Bryn Griffiths (Headmaster), Cicely Howells (Senior Mistress), Sybil Rees, Rhiannon Herbert, Margaret Phillips, Nan Peters (secretary). Second row: Beryl Davies, Pat Manley, Iris Thomas, May Spencer, Joe Owens, Varona Jones, Florence Morgan, Mona Bateman, John Bevan. Third row: Ben Phillips, Reginald Warlow, Gordon Parry, Colin Whittow, Dave Scourfield, Hugh Rees, Cyril Davies, Bertie Morgan. Back row: Dennis Hill, Eddie Steadman, Gordon Rayner, Bryn Samways, Ken Daniels, Mervyn Williams, Tommy Martin, Cliff Jenkins. With the introduction of comprehensive education in 1978 the school was renamed Sir Thomas Picton.

Seven

Churches and Chapels

The town is fortunate in having a number of churches whose architecture adds considerably to the stock of heritage buildings. Although St Martin's is the oldest church with its notable tapered spire close to the castle, it is St Mary's occupying a strategic position at the top of the High Street which is looked upon as the Town church and is a fine example of a medieval church with Early English, Decorated and Perpendicular features.

Nonconformity came to the town about the middle of the seventeenth century, the 'Green Meeting House' being first located on the Quay before moving to its site on St Thomas Green where the Albany United Reformed / Methodist church now stands. While all the major denominations are represented, Bethesda Baptist church and Tabernacle Congregational are excellent examples of different architectural styles which denote the importance of the town as a religious centre during the eighteenth and nineteenth centuries. One photograph (page 82) is of special interest since it shows what is reputed to have been the only Moravian church in Wales. It had an organ, brought from Bath by sea, on which Handel is supposed to have played! The building was demolished in 1961, and the organ was removed to Bethlehem chapel on the Cardigan road. Worthy of note, too, is the plaque at the entrance to the library in Dew Street commemorating the visit of John Wesley, then in his eighty-eighth year, on the last of his fourteen preaching visits to the town.

Maldwyn Thomas

An artistic view of St Thomas's church showing only the base of its massive thirteenth century tower. Its Norman origins are indicated by the great thickness of a section in its south wall.

An architect's drawing of the proposed alterations to St Mary's church following the removal of the steeple in 1802. Its oak-panelled roof is regarded as one of the finest in the country, and the church registers are the oldest in Pembrokeshire dating back to 1590.

The only Moravian church in Wales stood on St Thomas Green from 1773 until it closed in July 1957 and was subsequently demolished. Its last minister was the Revd George Harp who, before his appointment in 1954, was a missionary among the Eskimos in Labrador. The east end of the church, pictured above, is joined by a modest and rather unusual dwelling and, round the corner in Upper Market Street, was the Moravian Manse. The whole site was cleared in the 1960s and 1970s to make way for residential accommodation.

Boulston church. Today the church lies hidden in a thicket on the banks of the Western Cleddau, south of Boulston Manor. At high tide the waters lap the retaining wall of the churchyard. The walls to their full height, chancel arch, door and window apertures are all intact though the roof has long gone. It contains the Wogan tomb. Largely built in 1843 by Robert Ackland of Boulston Manor, the church was maintained until the 1930s when it was closed for worship.

The Vicar of St Martin's, the greatly revered Father Baring Gould, seated with his church choir around him at his last Patronal Festival in November 1954. He died seven months later aged 89 having served as vicar for 47 years. From left to right, back row: Charles Roach, Leslie Harris, John Fowles, Wyn Nicholson, Edgar John. Middle row: Clifford Phillips (organist for almost fifty years), Picton Codd, David Merriman, Lyn Jenkins, Ted James, William Phillips, Mansel Adams (choir-master). Front row: Billy Roach, Tom Drinning, George Morgan, Peter Merriman. Opposite: David Calvin-Thomas, Peter Drinning, Michael Jenkins, Maurice Jenkins, Maurice Sheppard (later to become President of the Royal Society of Watercolour Artists).

St David's church, Prendergast, from Sidney Rees Way (Prendergast relief road). It is of Norman origin; the medieval tower is over eight hundred years old. When it was rebuilt in 1868 (other than the tower), the architect, J. Foster of Bristol, was brother of the Rector, Revd F. Foster, who paid for the work on the church and the rectory out of his own pocket. Close to its porch and entrance is the grave of Howell Davies, often referred to as the 'Apostle of Pembrokeshire'. Members of the Stokes and Samson families of Scotchwells are also interred in the graveyard.

St Michael's church, Rudbaxton. This late twelfth or early thirteenth-century church contains a bust of General Sir Thomas Picton who was baptised here and fell at Waterloo, and the most remarkable funeral monument in Pembrokeshire, that of the Howard family of Flether Hill.

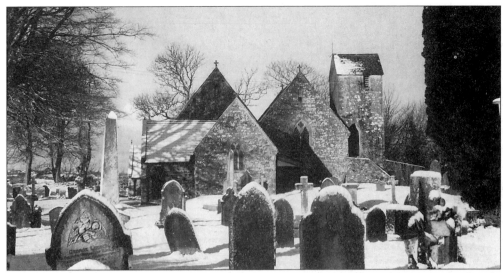

A snow-covered graveyard forms the foreground to the unique and beautiful St Ismael's church, Uzmaston. The ravages of dry and wet rot meant that all the pews and flooring had to be removed in 1991 and 1992. The carpeted interior and renovations together with new chairs allow varied seating arrangements to suit the different types of service. The church has two of the oldest bells in the country. When they were examined in 1980 the smaller of the two was found to have the inscription '+ MICHAEL : ARCHANGELVS'. The foundry mark suggested that it was cast in the Bristol foundry *c.* 1350. It has a diameter of $13\frac{1}{4}$ inches and weighs approximately $\frac{1}{2}$ cwt. The larger bell has the inscription 'SANCTE GABRYEL ORA PRO NOBIS'. It has a foundry mark suggesting it was also cast in the Bristol foundry *c.* 1410. It has a diameter of 26 inches and weighs between 4 and 5 cwt.

Tabernacle Congregational church was built in 1774 and restored in 1874 when the architects were Lawrence and Goodman. In its early years a number of its members were inclined to Calvinistic Methodism and Moravianism, but on their leaving the church *c.* 1790 it became a Congregational church. As a listed building it is much admired by residents and visitors. The plasterwork is reputed to be by Italian craftsmen.

Macphelah Baptist chapel in Portfield was built in 1824. It is now the subject of a demolition order to improve road visibility.

Bethesda Baptist church, built in 1878 by the Carmarthen architect George Morgan (1834-1915), one of the best-known chapel architects in Wales. It is in the Romanesque tradition, in hammer-dressed limestone, with Morgan's hallmark of round-headed windows and a fine central rose window.

Camrose Baptist chapel, built in 1838, is a typical example of the small nonconformist chapels to be found within a radius of three or four miles of the town. Unpretentious in appearance, this chapel was originally known as 'Lebanon' and celebrated its 150th anniversary at special commemorative services in 1988. It was first registered for marriages in 1901 and the first marriage was between James Bevan, Newgale Farm, and Elizabeth Hancock.

Hill Park Baptist church, built in 1888, was recently cleaned and tastefully redecorated. The architect was also George Morgan of Carmarthen who built Bethesda. The earlier chapel built in 1856 still remains on the adjoining site. This view in 1995 shows the underpass connecting it to the town centre and the Bridge Meadow.

Ebenezer Presbyterian church was built in 1817 and enlarged in 1844 and 1873 in the neo-classical manner. One of the smallest nonconformist chapels in the town, it now forms part of a pastorate which includes Millin chapel and Rehoboth in Hakin. The present minister, the Revd Raymond Webb was inducted to the joint pastorate in July 1991. Prior to that date the Revd Arwyn Thomas, formerly Moderator of the South Pembrokeshire Presbytery, was Pastor for a record breaking thirty-one years. Other loved and respected Pastors were the Revd William Mendus (1891-1920) followed by the Revds Ifor Jenkins and Lyndhurst Wales.

Albany chapel, founded in 1638, began with Quaker and dissenting associations and was known as The Green Meeting, i.e. The Meeting on The Green. Initially Independent, then Congregational, since 1985 Albany is jointly United Reformed/Methodist. It has never been possible to establish firmly the origin of its name but a tablet in the church proclaims it 'is the mother church of Nonconformity in this County'. (See also p. 114.)

Eight

Entertainment

As the county town, Haverfordwest has long been the centre of entertainment for the area. In the 1800s much of it was 'home spun'; spelling bees and penny readings were regular features with the occasional concert by artists perhaps displaying more enthusiasm than talent. By the turn of the century amateur choirs and bands were becoming fashionable and under the guidance of a few talented musicians their number increased appreciably. The inter-war years saw a significant improvement in their standard of performance which was largely due to dedicated conductors who inspired their groups to greater efforts and encouraged competitiveness by entering them in local eisteddfodau. The names of some of the conductors such as James Adams, Griffin Bishop, Jack Edwards, Eddie Jones, George Hughes and his wife Sybil Hughes, are still remembered with pride and affection. Throughout this period the churches and chapels of the town played an important part in fostering music and the dramatic arts as is evidenced by some of the photographs.

In the field of opera, the Haverfordwest Arts Club since 1948 had produced notable performances by its opera group which enjoyed a considerable following throughout the county. In 1982 the Haverfordwest Amateur Operatic Society was established and continued to produce very good performances. From 1949 until 1974, plays and reviews by the Haverfordwest Dramatic Society, first in the County Theatre and later in the Little Theatre, enjoyed great popularity.

In recent years the town's secondary schools have expanded the range of appreciation with their ambitious performances of traditional and modern musicals, while their orchestras and bands have astonished many by their capability and musicianship. Since the 1920s the cinema has been a centre of entertainment and the Palace at the top of Market Street and the Cinema de Luxe in St Mary Street were the forerunners in this medium. The opening of the County Theatre on the New Bridge in 1935 provided a spacious building which attracted audiences for nearly forty years. It was demolished in early 1980 to make way for council offices.

Bill Richards

The 'Haverford' dance orchestra c. 1930, playing at the Pembrokeshire Hunt ball. From left to right: Elfed Thomas, David Edmonds, Percy Thomas, Harry Walton, Jim Viggars, Miss Scales Lloyd, Joe Meredith.

Mr Jack Edwards with the Haverfordwest Ladies Choir after its success at the Fishguard Eisteddfod in 1922. As an excellent trainer, Mr Edwards was always in great demand and was the conductor of numerous church and school choirs which gave memorable performances on most of the town's stages. From left to right, front row: May Wilkins, Dilys Williams, Maybro Phillips, Violet Owens, Ethel McKenzie, Pye John, Alice Owen. Second row: Lilian John, Brucie Phillips, Miss Jefferson, Lisa Jane Evans, Lilly Davies, Mrs Harry Morgan, Margaret Roberts, Dreda Pugh, Gladys Watson. The back row includes: Miss Edwards, Lottie Oliver, Mr Edwards, Mrs Edwards, Mary Baggott, Muriel Griffiths, Mabel Warlow and Charles Oliver, secretary.

Students of Mrs Eaden's School of Art, Upper Market Street c. 1920. From left to right, front row: Margaret Roberts, Peggy Roberts, Alice Griffiths, Nora Hammond, Anne Roberts, Margaret Eaden, Doris Hammond, Janie Thomas, Nanny Sweeney. Back row: -?-, -?-, Lawton Davies, KKK, Birt Llewellin, Gordon Llewellin. The fancy dress ball organised annually by Mrs Eaden was first held in the Masonic Hall but was so successful that it moved to a larger venue in St Mary's Assembly Hall. Attendance was by invitation only and fancy dress was obligatory. From c. 1922 it was called the Arts Ball.

The St Martin's Players with the cast of the operetta *Cupid and the Ogre* performed in the Masonic Hall in April 1936. Interestingly, one of the cast, Clifford Moses (second row, third from right) later became a professional actor. In the same row, fifth from left, is Father Baring Gould's daughter, Mrs Dora Waters, who was at that time over from America. Amateur dramatic productions by the various town churches were commonplace during the 1920s and into the 1940s.

Some of the Haverfordwest Male Voice Choir before their last concert with Eddie Jones, 27 October 1946. From left to right, seated: Dilys Thomas, Dorothy Williams, Eddie Jones, Violet Owen, Elsie Bollom, and George Evans.

Princess Ida, one of Gilbert and Sullivan's lesser-known works selected for the twentieth autumn production in 1968 by the Opera Group of the Haverfordwest Arts Club. Produced and directed by Mrs Sybil Hughes and staged at the County Secondary School, it proved an excellent choice and was greatly enjoyed by audiences at all three performances. The cast, from left to right, kneeling: Violet Snook, Gwyneth John, Lynne Thomas, Margaret Robinson, Margaret Miles, Dorothy Williams, Janet Morris, Sheila Morris, Mary Hay, Jean Rees, John Davies, June Phillips, Moira Perkins, Susan Thomas, Vera Hughes, Sheila Cook, Anne Burnett.

Second row: Doris Price, Helen Phillips, Vesta Davies, Olwen Thomas, John Cook, Barbara Thomas, Vernon Evans, Islwyn Perkins, Iris Thomas, Josie Jenkins, Dorothy James, Dorothy Lloyd, John Diamond, Dorothy Thomas, Nancy Rees, Maureen Hunt. Back row: Norman Jenkins, Bill Morris, Frank Morgan, Doug Hewitson, Malcolm Thomas, Bryn Lewis, Hugh Thomas, Bill Lloyd, Peter Thomas, James Kilroy, Albert Jones, Derek Brock, David Hughes, Noel Rees, Tom Townsend, Tom Lamb, Victor John, Phillip Thomas.

Haverfordwest YFC Annual Ball at the Masonic Hall on 9 November 1960. From left to right, front row: Peter Jenkins, Sheila Belton, Valerie Thomas, Margot Belton, Susan Rees, Diane Rees, Betty Roch, Margaret Philpin. Second row: David Morgan, Gillian Evans, Josephine Evans, June Lawrence, Rosemary Bowler, Margaret John, Betty Roch, Margaret Davies. Third row: Revd Ivor Rees (joint leader), Rex Jenkins, Dilys Dowling, David Evans, Barbara Edwards, Barbara Morgan. Fourth row: Billy Scriven, Denzil Edwards, Ellis Jones, Walter Roch. Back row: Martin Richards (joint leader), John Allen, Arthur George, Gwyn Jones, Kemsley Mathias, John Morgan, Fred Jenkins, George Hancock.

Haverfordwest Young Farmers Club, the winning team in the County knockout quiz competition. In the final round on 18 April 1962 they beat Tenby YFC to win the silver trophy presented by the Regent Oil Co. From left to right: Ellis Jones, Barbara Allen, Graham Roberts, Sheila Belton (captain), Billy Scriven, Mr Griffiths (area representative for Regent), and David Evans.

Haverfordwest YFC folk dance team at the annual YFC rally at Bush Grammar School, Pembroke in May 1960. 'As usual, the folk dancing was popular and hundreds of people crowded into the main hall to see Clynderwen win the Daniel Daniel Challenge Cup'. Haverfordwest was third. From left to right: Barbara Edwards, Arthur George, Susan Rees, George Hancock, June Lawrence, John Pritchard, Betty Roch, Walter Roch, Betty Roch, Gwyn Jones, Valerie Thomas, Rex Jenkins.

Haverfordwest Male Voice Choir at its annual dinner, 7 January 1972, with three of the conductors present. From left to right, seated: Lewis Williams (Conductor 1960-66), Mrs Molly Griffiths (Accompanist), Ivor Rowlands (Chairman), Mrs E. M. Davies (Conductor), Bill Price (Conductor 1956-60), Howard Davies (oldest chorister). Second row: John Hughes, Glyn Thomas, David Thomas, Hylton John, Fred Jacks, Bryn Lewis, Bertie Davies, Glan Lewis, Arthur John, Deryk Brock, Watcyn Richards, Hywel Rees, Bill Baker, John Reynish, Ellis Hughes, -?-, Billy Watts, Tom Rowlands, Ynyr Evans, Malcom Thomas, Calvin Jones, Len Dixon, Bill Morris, Billy Owen. Back row: Ivor Davies, Larry Coleman, Selwyn Morgan, Peter Williams, Gwynne Warlow (Secretary/Treasurer), Frank Morgan, Derek Rees. 1996 witnessed the centenary of the Haverfordwest Male Voice Choir. During that time it has delighted countless thousands by its stirring singing of traditional choruses, hymns and popular songs. While the county town would rightly wish to claim it as its own, its choristers come from many corners of the county.

Jack Holt's Dance Band in 1949, playing at a Pembrokeshire War Agricultural Committee dance in the Drill Hall. From left to right: Ivor Phillips (accordion), Jim Day (master of ceremonies), John Cousins (saxophone), Madge Davies (vocalist), Jack Holt (drums), Danny Williams (trumpet), Ken Shaw (piano), George Merritt (trombone).

The Glan Cleddau dancers at the Fishguard Eisteddfod in 1986 where they were placed second in their group. They were formed to compete in the 1972 National Eisteddfod held in Haverfordwest. They aim to promote Welsh folk dancing and to keep alive the traditional folk dances of Wales with tuition to groups (for example, the YFC) and schools. From left to right, kneeling: Teleri Palmer, Ann Sambrook, Elizabeth George, Ann Morris, Christine Petts, Margaret Redpath. Second row: Rhiannon Herbert, Huw Davies, Judith Williams, Jean Rees, Mary Hay, Morwel Palmer. Back row: Geoff Warrington, David Rye, Brian Perkins, Geraint Evans, Vernon Petts, Leslie Morris, Simon Richardson, Olive Evans, Jill Hay, Carol Williams, Derek Griffiths, Siân Williams, Jo Williams.

The County Youth Band with its conductor, Mr Joffre Swales MBE, in front of St Mary's church, Haverfordwest. The band won the gold medal in the Boosey and Hawkes South Wales and West of England Regional Band Festival in 1990. In the following year the band was again an award winner in the Wales and the Marches National Concert Band Festival.

The Mary Immaculate Band was received by Pope John Paul II in front of St Peter's, Rome, in May 1981. The conductor, Mr Joffre Swales, is being greeted by His Holiness while Father McGreal, Mr Ernst Herman (Chairman of the band), and several of the young players look on admiringly. It was the first outdoor audience to be arranged by the Pontiff who faced an attempt on his life only a few months later.

Haverfordwest Male Voice Choir at St Mary's church, 5 February 1988. From left to right, seated: Glan Thomas, Ifor Swales, John Feehan, Bill Morris, Gwyn Griffiths (conductor), Seimon Morris (accompanist), John Hughes, Arthur Brady, John Williams, Gwynne Warlow. Second row: Bill Clow, Keith Rogers, Jack Campbell, Roy Lewis, Bill Millar, Roger Jones, Gordon Morris, Joe Evans, Peter Kinsey, John Percey, Ynyr Evans, Gwyn Bunston. Third row: Nic Wonnacott, David Irving, Vaughan Jenkins, Ian Hunter, Mel Jenkins, Roy Bryant, Deryk Brock, Bryn Lewis, Arwel Phillips, Russ Gould, Malcolm Thomas, Trevor Hughes, Derek Watts, David Devonald. Back row: Richard Hellon, Bob Hughes, Phil Morgan, Eric John, Derek Rees, Dai Harries, Watcyn Richards, Colin Rogers, Eifion John, Bill Donovan, Bill Baker.

At first glance, few people would associate music, drama and the arts with this drab building. However, it is, in fact, the Little Theatre, the home of the Haverfordwest Dramatic Society, formed in 1949. By dint of tremendous enthusiasm and hard work, the Little Theatre stalwarts converted the interior of this former malthouse on the Mariners Square into a warm, comfortable centre and from 1953 until 1974 they produced a large number of dramas, comedies and revues which delighted audiences. Many of the revues, especially those by Trevor Jones, were purely local and based on Haverfordwest events and people. These shows were enormously successful and were repeated many times – and Haverfordwest people continued to be amazed at the talent that lay in their midst!

Nine

Halls, Houses and Castles

The countryside surrounding Haverfordwest, the county town, is rich in buildings of size and antiquity reflecting almost a thousand years of Pembrokeshire's history. The earliest structures are the Norman castles ranging from the simple earth works such as Camrose and New Moat to the later stone affairs which with continual habitation developed from a purely military function into more refined domestic buildings. Picton Castle, home to the Philipps family demonstrates this as does Carew Castle with its range of oriel windows created by Sir John Perrot. He, of course, is synonymous with Haverfordwest and is also associated with a later great house, Haroldston, now in ruins but once 'ornamented with groves' where pheasants were originally introduced to the country.

By the eighteenth century a Pembrokeshire gentleman demanded more than a jumbled collection of medieval buildings that had sufficed for his ancestors. He was looking for 'prospects' and elegance. Old Boulston, for example, right on the waterside, was not rebuilt, rather a new mansion was built on higher ground with views down over the old ruins. Many older house,s if not pulled down or re-sited, were extended and improved, Scolton, New Moat, Dumpledale, Tregwynt and Pentypark are all examples. The grander families also maintained town houses in Haverfordwest, Goat Street having solid examples belonging to Philipps of Picton, Scourfield of Williamston and the finest, Foley House, being connected to the Foley or Fawly family of Ridgeway near Llawhaden.

Many successful business and professional men from Haverfordwest aspired to the tradition of buying a country house and estate. Avellenau near the town was built in 1845 by a solicitor William Evans, whose successors, the Eaton Evans, lived there for many years. Dr David Evans built Treffgarn Hall in 1824 and his family remained there until 1914. William Owen, architect, builder and entrepreneur in the town actually built several country houses near Haverfordwest including Glanafon, Scolton and Cottesmore. Having made his fortune he decided to buy for himself Poyston and Withybush, both ancient houses which he improved.

David Ellis

Poyston, seen from across the lake in this photograph from the 1884 album of George Leader Owen of Withybush. It was home to the Picton family, the most famous member of which was General Sir Thomas Picton who, after a distinguished military career, fell at Waterloo. It later became home to William Owen who lived in the house in 1859 when he served as High Sheriff. Later it was the home of his son, Dr Henry Owen, the scholarly local historian whose late nineteenth-century library is a fine feature of the house.

Kensington House, Tower Hill in 1955. This was the Haverfordwest home of Lord Kensington and it is reputed that in the early nineteenth century Lady Kensington was responsible for the demolition of St Mary's spire, fearing that it might fall on the house. It was considered to be one of the finest gentry houses in the town and before being demolished c. 1960 it was used as an annex to nearby Taskers School. The site is now a car park for the registry office.

St Brides was built for Lord Kensington at the beginning of the 1830s and earlier photographs show quite a graceful, symmetrical castellated mansion with tall extension pipes to raise the height of the chimneys, the latter suggesting that the splendidly exposed position was not without problems. At the end of the nineteenth century considerable work was carried out, giving the building a heavier appearance as shown in this 1975 photograph. For many years after the First World War the mansion served as a hospital, as did Sealyham. In recent years it has been well converted as a Holiday Bond property.

Foley House in Goat Street in 1955. It was one of Haverfordwest's fine old residences and the home of several distinguished families over the years. It was designed and built in 1794 by John Nash, the celebrated architect, on the order of Richard Foley, a leading Pembrokeshire public figure and brother of Admiral Sir Thomas Foley GCB, one of Lord Nelson's famous captains. Sir Thomas was a regular visitor to Foley House and in August 1802 he was accompanied by Lord Nelson who received a tremendous welcome from the townspeople. Town houses for the gentry gradually fell out of fashion and in the late 1950s Foley House was purchased by Pembrokeshire County Council. Eventually it was converted to its present use as offices of the Pembrokeshire Justices Clerks Department. Below: the north front of Foley House in 1985 from the car park, formerly the garden. John Nash's early classical simplicity is displayed at its best in Richard Foley's urban villa.

The Masonic Hall, opened in 1872, is one of the town's few neo-classical buildings, and forms a striking feature of Picton Place.

Dale Castle. Historic home of the Lloyd-Philipps family, this imposing castellated building nestles into a gentle south-facing hillside of the valley that lies behind Dale village and close to the landing place of Henry Tudor on his way to Bosworth. Although the castle has been extensively remodelled, like many local mansions it incorporates early sections.

Scotchwells House. Admiral John Lort Stokes stands beside his carriage with Mrs Stokes and the coachman, the latter wearing the appropriate livery. The photograph is believed to date from 1876 and shows interesting detail such as the Victorian conservatory and the trellis (to secure creepers) on the wall behind the porch. St Botolphs and Cuffern were both houses that belonged to the Stokes family.

Scotchwells House in 1986. Superficially a nineteenth-century house, it incorporates earlier sections and is most famous as the home of the explorer of Western Australia and New Zealand, Admiral Stokes, who was born and eventually died in the house. It was later the home of Mr Louis Samson and his family. His son, Sir Edward Marley Samson, was a distinguished lawyer and political figure.

'Around Haverfordwest we find even now a goodly number of mansions fit to environ a county town, and form the materials of a refined circle of society' wrote the genealogist Thomas Nicholas in 1872. This view of Withybush around 1880, from the album of George Leader Owen whose home it was, illustrates one of the houses Nicholas lists.

Cottesmore. This beautifully situated mansion with its view down the Cleddau valley was built by Edward Massey in 1841 on the site of the earlier house, formerly known as 'the Cotts', and occupied by his father-in-law Jonathan Peel. Probably designed and built by the ubiquitous William Owen, its interesting siting of the two main chimney stacks is a feature well known in Ireland and may reflect Massey's Irish connections. It remains a well-cared-for home.

Avellenau, *c.* 1870, when the house was leased by John and Sarah Dawkins (he was the Dawkins of Greenish & Dawkins, owners of the Market Street department store, Commerce House). The house, built for solicitor William Evans by William Owen in 1845 (shortly before Owen built the Corn Market) reverted to its owners in the late 1880s and was the home of the Eaton Evans family for many years. The handsome house looks much now as it did then but it is presently uninhabited.

Williamston House, the home of the Scourfield family, formerly of Moat at New Moat, is a rambling house of Victorian appearance like Scotchwells and which similarly incorporates earlier features. The owner at the beginning of the present century, Sir Owen Scourfield (son of the MP for the Borough of Haverfordwest and from 1868 for the County of Pembroke), was an enthusiast in many fields including cattle breeding, rifle shooting and motoring. The mansion was the venue for an early Pembrokeshire motor rally. Sir Owen was also known for his obsessive fascination with railway timetables.

Haroldston, historic home of the Perrot family is now a sadly ruined complex of buildings which has been much diminished even in recent years. Enough remains, however, to give some idea of what the late medieval mansion was like. Pictured here is the Steward's Tower as it was as recently as 1984. The undisturbed grounds form the important site of a Tudor garden. Not many miles away, across the western Cleddau, the early riverside mansion of the Wogan family at Boulston lies in a similarly decayed state.

Picton Castle. One of Wales' most historic houses and home to the Philipps family. It has particular links with Haverfordwest and St Mary's church especially. The core of this mansion is a medieval castle, the form of its four towers still absolutely visible despite centuries of extensive adaptation, culminating in the addition of a castellated west wing, added by the first Lord Milford about the beginning of the nineteenth century, followed later by a 'Norman' porch and a handsome stable block.

Camrose House, formerly the home of the Webb-Bowen family from 1801 until 1918 when Captain Lewis Penn succeeded to the estate. It is a fine eighteenth-century house with some later alterations. As well as its distinctive arched windows it has a handsome staircase and the unusual feature of a motte in the grounds.

Glanafon. Built about 1839, almost certainly by William Owen, for Jonathan Haworth Peel (cousin of Sir Robert Peel) who had just sold his former home, Cottesmore, to his son-in-law Edward Massey, a member of a distinguished Anglo-Irish family. A slightly austere house, of late Georgian character despite its later date, it resembles Scolton, a known William Owen house. It remains a family home in excellent repair.

Butterhill, near St Ishmaels, was the home of the Roch family (George Roch was High Sheriff in 1841). Though now derelict, it is typical of the quite large number of small mansions and large farmhouses, some of considerable antiquity, that are to be found around Pembrokeshire and in most cases the social life of their owners would have centred on Haverfordwest. Butterhill, like Cuffern, is one of the double-pile form of building, much favoured for larger houses in south-west Wales from the early eighteenth century.

Sandy Haven, photographed from the north *c.* 1990. This much-altered house reveals its early character, which is not so obvious from other aspects. In 1557 and 1687 the owner was High Sheriff, an indication that the house enjoyed high status over many years. Many houses in the county display early features which often remain unrecognised.

Ten

People and Places

People and places are the principal ingredients of history. All other categories fall in behind these general headings as natural corollaries.

Both people and places provide a telling picture of what life was like in the past, giving an insight into social conditions, sartorial styles and fashions, living standards, recreational and cultural activities, dietary regimes, personal hygiene and religious influences. Retrospective glances bear telling testimony to how people and places have changed and each examination of a detailed photograph highlights new information. In the 1912 photograph of the unveiling of the William Nichol memorial below, my wife identified among the sea of faces her great-grandfather and an uncle while I recognised a former St Mary's church chorister and employee of Bland's garage.

The photographs in this section take us from the dawn of the Edwardian era to the new Elizabethan period, now more than forty years old. Older readers will see familiar faces and places and will experience their own personal memories of voices, mannerisms and character quirks, while younger ones will look back at the unknown and completely different world of their parents and grandparents. The personalities featured here made a significant contribution to the life of the county town, each fitting his or her particular piece of the jigsaw into place. Whatever the perspective, looking back is a fascinating exercise.

Derek Rees

This Balmoral red-granite column situated at the junction of High Street and Dark Street was erected as a memorial to William Nichol in 1912. The inscription reads: 'The noble army of Martyrs praise Thee'. On this spot William Nichol of this town, was burnt at the stake For the Truth, April 9th 1558'. Little is known about the young man other than he laid down his life for the Protestant faith in which he so strongly believed. About 1925, during road excavations in High Street, a hole was uncovered about thirteen metres from the site of the memorial. It was fifteen centimetres square and nearly a metre deep and is probably the spot where the stake was erected.

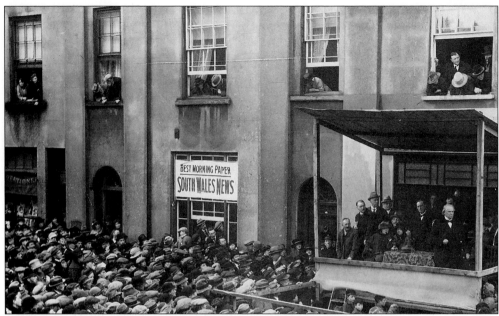

This photograph appeared in a local paper in November 1922 with the caption: 'Mr Lloyd George addressing some thousands of people in Castle Square, Haverfordwest, in support of the candidature of his son, Major Gwilym Lloyd George, who is standing as a National Liberal for the Pembroke Division.' It was the first time he stood for Pembrokeshire and, with one break from October 1924 to May 1929 when the Conservative MP was Major C.W.M. Price, he was Liberal MP until February 1950. Local personalities on the platform include, from left to right: Cllr Richard Sinnett; Mr Rees (Narberth), the Liberal agent; Mr Sidney Rees and the candidate. Seated at the table are Mrs Margaret Lloyd George, daughter Megan, and former Liberal MP, Sir Evan Jones. Looking down from the windows are the families who lived above their businesses in Victoria Place: No. 1 – Mr Francis Phillips, chemist; No. 3 – Mr Fred J. Warren, accountant; No. 5 – Mr Edwin John, stationer.

Marjorie Lovell (1889-1979) in a study by Alfred Eagers. 'Got any baccy my love?' was her common request and she was rarely seen without her stump of a clay pipe. Probably the best known of Pembrokeshire travelling hawkers, familiar throughout the length and breadth of the county, inseparable from her pony and trap. Born in Herefordshire, she moved to Pembrokeshire with her parents when she was three weeks old. In spite of her appearance she was reputed to be a lady of some wealth with property in Carmarthen. In later years she lived in a caravan at Withybush where she died.

Opposite: Mr and Mrs Sydney Dawkins and family on the lawn at Haylett Grange c. 1920, with the family's Overland car behind. Mr Dawkins was prominent in public life and was President of the Pembrokeshire Agricultural Society in 1906. An advert in the *Pembroke County Guardian* in 1921 extols the qualities of the Overland car imported from USA: 'Price Complete £395. Completely equipped, including Electric Starter and Lighting Set – Buy Now! Overland Sales in Wales for June for cars only, 469, and Dealers still waiting for more – Lady Owner Driver says 2,197 miles without a puncture – This is truly the Economy Car!'

Haverfordwest Wings For Victory Group at the opening ceremony of 'Wings For Victory' week, 15 May 1943. From left to right, seated: Miss M. Ellis (Mayoress); Major Gwilym Lloyd George MP; Ald. L.H. Ellis (Mayor); Mrs Lloyd George; Lady Jones. Back row: Revd A. Baring Gould (Vicar of St Martin's and Mayor's Chaplain); Mr F.R. Lowther; Squadron Leader A. Watts; Mr Stuart Williams (Assistant Savings Commissioner); and Sir Evan D. Jones, President of the Week, and previously MP for Pembrokeshire (1918-1922). 'The Week began when Major Lloyd George addressed a large gathering outside the Shire Hall… Previously they had been guests of the Mayor at lunch served in the War Workers Canteen in Rosemary Lane'. Across Hill Street was Hill House College where this photograph was taken; note the tape on the window panes – a wartime precaution against flying glass splinters.

An audience of nearly two thousand packed the Market Hall on the evening of Saturday 10 April 1954 when Clement Attlee, Leader of the Labour Party, and his wife appeared on the platform to support the Labour MP, Desmond Donnelly. From left to right: Lord and Lady Kenswood, Mr Bob Rees, Mrs Eunice Williams, Miss Bronwen Davies, Mrs Attlee, Mr Trevor Evans, Mr Attlee, Mr Walter Fish (President of the Pembrokeshire Constituency Labour Party), Mrs Gwen Parry, Mr Donnelly, Mr Tom Parry (Labour Party agent). Before the arrival of the speakers there was singing by the Llangwm and District Ladies Choir.

Major and Mrs Jack Higgon, Scolton; Mr Jim Jones, kennel huntsman; and Mr and Mrs Kenneth Walker, Boulston at a meet of the Pembrokeshire Hunt, Haroldston Ruins, 1938-39. Major Higgon was appointed Master in 1938 but with the outbreak of the Second World War rejoined his regiment, the Welsh Guards. After the war he continued as Master for one year and was succeeded by Mr Kenneth Walker. The beech trees in the background were felled during the war and the wood manufactured locally into soles for clogs.

'Sportsmen All'. Well-known personalities and supporters of the Pembrokeshire Hunt outside the Mariners Hotel c. 1950. Front row: Billy Munt, Captain Lewis Penn, 'Marvel', Major W. Sandford Evans ('Titch'). Back row: Russell Jones, Mrs Audrey George, Tom George, Harold Hedley (who owned the 'Mariners'), David George, Geoff Keppel-Palmer, -?-. 'Marvel', so-called because to him everything was 'a marvel', was a very well-known farrier whose forge was at Cromwell Corner. Not everyone knew his correct name (Harry John) and cheques were sometimes made out to Mr Marvel.

The Royal British Legion Committee on the Bridge Meadow one Sunday morning in 1947. This group was the nucleus of the Entertainment Committee which organised dances at the Market Hall and concerts at the County Theatre for the benefit of causes supported by the RBL. From left to right, seated: Harold Arran (Scolton Villas), Tom Lamb (Merlins Crescent), Dilly Carr (Caretakers House, County Offices), Jimmy Nicholas (Bush Row), Albert Morris (Cleddau Avenue). Middle row: Tom Brace (Prendergast), Leslie Absalom (Market Street), Claude Davies (Bridgend Square), David Evans (Albert Street), George Havard (Portfield). Back row: Archie Evans (Cartlett), Albert Thomas (Barn Street), George Nicholls (Gloucester Terrace), Charles Oliver (Prendergast), Jack Lewis (Prendergast Place).

Alderman Claude Davies (1879-1967), Mayor and Admiral of the Port of Haverfordwest in 1954-55. Alderman Davies, a coal merchant, was elected to the Town Council in November 1945 and served for many years. He was in the forces throughout the First World War, was awarded the Military Medal and was subsequently a leading member of the British Legion in Haverfordwest. Straightforward yet kindly, he enjoyed much respect, especially for the strictly fair way in which he conducted his extensive coal merchant's business during the desperate fuel shortage immediately after the Second World War.

Opposite: The minister's induction at Albany Congregational church, now United Reformed/Methodist, with the deacons in 1921. From left to right, seated: Revd David Walters (Moderator, Wales); Revd Myrddin J. Jones; S.P. Morris. Standing: Arthur Thomas, William Wheeler, William Thomas, Alfred H. James, Chas. C. Saies.

Haverfordwest had many public walks in former days, one of the most popular being that leading up to Scotchwells House, the home of the Marley Sampson family, where two young strollers in 1955 are being led along the rugged path by a friendly goose.

'Sized up' and on parade at the 1949 County Fire Brigade Annual Competition held on St Thomas Green. From left to right: David Evans, regular fireman, and part-timers Ronnie James, Tom Nicholls, Joe Freeney and George Edwards, Mayor of Milford Haven 1996-97.

116

The appellation 'Mr Music' is well deserved for Joffre Swales who was awarded the MBE in 1975 for his services to the cause of music in the town for over fifty years. Returning to his home town after serving in the Royal Marines during the Second World War he set about enabling young people to learn a wind instrument and then playing in the Mary Immaculate Band and later in the County Youth Band. His skill as a player and teacher of so many instruments is proverbial and there are many young (and not so young!) musicians today who remember with gratitude his skilled teaching and encouraging words. Now in his eighties, he is still conducting and able to lead the band along the streets of 'Honey Harfat' which trumpets its appreciation of what he has achieved over so many years. In 1987 he was immensely proud to be presented with the Soviet Medal for service on the Russian convoys in 1941 and 1942.

Mr G. Douglas James (1884-1977) was born and bred in the town and his writings on its history, its characters and its institutions were a labour of love. His book, *The Town and County of Haverfordwest and its Story*, published in 1958 and now sadly out of print, remains the only comprehensive history of the town. He taught English in the Grammar School, but despite his graduate education and his erudition, proudly retained his 'Harfat' accent and was down-to-earth and unassuming. He loved the local dialect and made frequent use of its colloquialisms. During an exposition of the work of John Buchan to his Grammar School pupils one day, he suddenly broke off on noticing woodlice radiating to all corners of the classroom, having been released from a jam jar by a mischievous boy. Forgetting the lesson and reverting to his best 'Harfat' accent, he queried: 'Who let these penny sows out in here?'. His contribution to the town's historical heritage is immense.

A view from the tower of St Thomas' church in March 1954 showing the town in a state of post-war change. With Hermons Hill House in the left foreground and the intrusive bulk of the County Theatre beyond; Prospect Place and the fast developing Queensway; Sir Thomas Picton School; but the Government Building has not yet been built at Cherry Grove. An interesting detail is the double-decker bus at the old Green's Garage to the right of the picture.

The Minister, Revd T. Arwyn Thomas (seated), with the Elders of Millin chapel at the Commemorative Centenary Service in 1966. From left to right: Richie Owen, Harry Morgan, William Morgan, Meidrim Evans, Ronnie Evans, Stanley Nicholas, Willie Owen, C.B. James.

The re-hallowing of St Ismael's church, Uzmaston, on 16 June 1962 following restoration. From left to right, seated: Canon William Watkins, Vicar of Uzmaston; Rt. Revd J. Ivor Rees, Lord Bishop of St Davids; Ven. John Harvey. Standing: Mr Frank Gill, Revds Paul Morgans, Jonathan Lean, Timothy Hewitt, Geoffrey Gwyther, Roger White, Roger Jones, Arwyn Thomas, Paul Davies, Canon Howell Fuller, Canon Peter Edwards, Mr John Milne.

The main entrance to the old County War Memorial Hospital at Winch Lane, Haverfordwest in 1957. This remarkable institution was built and maintained for many years between the wars by voluntary subscriptions and funds raised by a variety of social and sporting events. The surgical, medical and nursing care it offered to Pembrokeshire people was second to none and there was genuine regret everywhere when the hospital lost its voluntary status with the advent of the National Health Service in 1948.

Haverfordwest's noted Town Crier, Mr Dai Morris, heading a town carnival procession in 1965. Dai loved the office of Town Crier and revelled in the dressing-up and general paraphernalia of the ancient office. Although he did not have a very powerful voice he made his announcements with tremendous gusto, especially the preliminary 'Oyez, Oyez, Oyez,' and took no notice whatever when small boys (and some adults) standing around would sometimes reply 'O No, O No'. Dai regarded his duties seriously and often took part in a national town criers' contest organised by a Sunday newspaper in one of the old English towns.

Reputedly one of the first petrol pumps in Haverfordwest. Mr Teddy Nicholas and Miss Florrie Robbins outside Trafalgar House, Hill Street. College Court now occupies this site.

A group of Mason Arms 'regulars' in the early 1950s prior to a coach trip to Porthcawl. Recognised from left to right: bus driver Tom Adams (Narberth), Joe Williams, Bert Rees, Joe Potter, Reggie Slate, David Davies, George Thomas, Jack Davies (wearing cap), Leslie Devonald, Jack Hayes, Alan Williams, Jimmy Reynolds (trilby), George Reynolds, Ted Collins (landlord), Albert Evans, Clifford Williams, Roy Bennett, Harry Bennett (cap), Phil Evans, Fred Evans (cap), Tommy Cole, Bertie Williams, Bill Gunn, Tommy Reader, Ivor Barrah.

James Day's 'South Wales Cokernut Throwing stall' at Portfield Fair, St Thomas Green, early 1900s.

The railway came to Haverfordwest at the end of 1853 and a short time later was extended to Neyland and Milford Haven. It crossed the River Cleddau by means of a Brunel-designed wooden viaduct (replaced about the turn of the century by the present structure). Both opened to allow the passage of shipping, upon which the town and district so largely depended at that time. The railway revolutionised Haverfordwest as a business, cultural and social centre and for over a hundred years contributed immeasurably to the general prosperity of the town and district. The town's importance as a port gradually disappeared and vessels no longer came up the river. Eventually the railway also began to lose its vital role, a development regarded with regret by many in the town, especially those of the older generation.

Eleven

Transport

The pattern of transportation in and around Haverfordwest developed little in the eighteenth and the first half of the nineteenth century, being limited to horse-drawn coaches and wagons and the great use of the river.

This changed dramatically when the town was joined to the railway network in 1853 which greatly increased the distance that could be travelled in a day and offered the much greater convenience of transporting large quantities of goods. While the early carriages were open, with little protection from the elements, relatively fast long-distance travel now became available to a much larger section of the population than ever before.

This new found independence was enhanced further in the last decades of the nineteenth century by the invention of the internal combustion engine, and following that, the creation of the horseless carriage or motor car as it later became known. In the early days motoring was restricted to the wealthier sections of society as cars tended to be large and expensive, but by the 1920s smaller less expensive vehicles were being manufactured by new mass production methods thus bringing them within the reach of business people and farmers of the locality. Scheduled bus services by Green's Motors and later Western Welsh, provided an essential service for school children and people travelling to work in Haverfordwest, especially from Milford Haven and Neyland. Many also travelled into town from Clarbeston Road and Neyland by train.

Whereas the River Cleddau provided the main means of transporting goods for hundreds of years it also determined where the earliest settlement took place, being the lowest crossing point on the river. The introduction of the railway system had only a minor impact on the structure of Haverfordwest. Sadly the same cannot be said about the motor car which has brought great changes to the appearance of the town.

Alan Bland

The Fishguard Mail cart with driver, George George c. 1911. For the journeys to Fishguard and Milford, a team of two horses was used but for the runs to St Davids, 'with sixteen miles and seventeen hills', a team of four horses was needed.

Mr John Andrew Bland, accompanied by Mr Ernie Holt, at the wheel of his 1909 15-hp Rover, registration number DE 199.

Mr Jack Nicholas with the Judge's valet in the Castle Square.

124

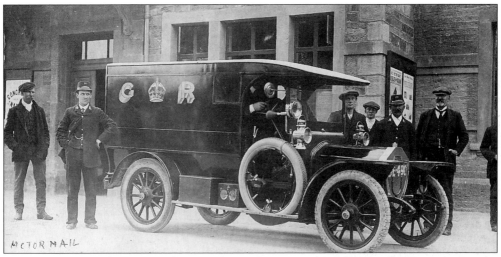

Before the days of the red post office van the mail service was run by Bland's. Here awaiting the mail at Haverfordwest station on 7 June 1914 is the first motor mail van to operate from Haverfordwest to the Fishguard ferry. With the van are, from left to right: -?-, Postman Gilbert Griffiths (Prendergast) and brother of local photographer Seth Griffiths, Jack Hines (driver), Tom Hines (Cartlett), the foreman at Blands who joined the firm from the Rover Motor Company, Lewis 'Hellcat' Morgan (Prendergast), Postman Jones (Milford Road), J.A. Bland. The registration number was DE 490, a green 15-hp Rover first registered on 30 May 1914 for mail transport from Haverfordwest to Goodwick. A mechanic was on duty in the garage every night to service the van for the following morning.

An Albion charabanc owned by Mr Hughes, Freystrop, and driven by Mr Cousins, also of Freystrop, with a choir outing in 1924. 'State-of-the-art' at the time with acetylene lamps, solid tyres, 'robust suspension' and a canvas top which, with all the passengers helping, took twenty minutes to erect, and a propensity to need passengers' assistance up hills when it tended to boil enthusiastically.

The *Resolute* leaves the gasworks quay with a choir outing *c.* 1905; she also did duty as the weekly market boat though many people came to town by donkey and pony and trap.

The 'up platform' at Haverfordwest railway station, *c.* 1900, with ample space left by narrowing the gauge from Brunel's seven-foot in 1884. Passengers are waiting for the 10.40 to Paddington for which the first-class return fare was £3. 12. 3*d.*

A Green's Motors bus outside the Horse and Jockey, Steynton, with the driver, Mr Ernie Holt. The bus DE 3886 is a Dodge, with the body possibly built by Green's Motors in their Quay Street workshop.

Hill climb on Arnold's Hill when the road was closed to the public. The car DE 1902, is a Rover 12 hp, registered April 1920. The driver, thought to be Mr Francis Phillips of The Dingle, Crundale, was a director of the Welch Autocar Co. with Mr Eric Green as his passenger.

Acknowledgements

The Haverfordwest Civic Society wishes to thank everyone who has given encouragement and support in the preparation of this publication Haverfordwest. Photographs have appeared from attics and drawers to see daylight for the first time in decades. Sometimes, names and occasions have been known but in many cases extensive research has been necessary to provide the story behind the picture. It is particularly gratifying that so many members and friends became engrossed in the challenge to know 'who?' 'when?' and 'where?'. We hope that they will see it was time well spent!

Limited space makes it difficult to acknowledge everyone but special recognition should be made of the help received from John Owen, County Archivist, and his staff at the Pembrokeshire Record Office, and Mrs Anita Thomas, Reference and Local Studies Librarian, with her staff in the Haverfordwest Reference Library. We were fortunate to have people with such patience and expertise available to help us.

We wish to acknowledge our indebtedness to approximately 70 members and friends who generously entrusted us with the loan of over 300 photographs from which 219 were finally selected for publication. They are attributed by page number and 'a' (above) or 'b' (below). Where both photographs on a page are lent by the same person, 'a' and 'b' are omitted.

David Banner (46a, 48a); Ron Batte (78b); Alan and June Bland (59b, 94a, 123, 124, 125a); Thora Bowler (54b); Helen Danzey (80b); Willie Davies (52b); Alfred Eagers (111); James Eaton-Evans (32, 33); John Evans (106b); Mair Evans (95a); Margaret Evans (74a); Olive Evans (71a, 121b); Revd Christopher Gillam (85b); Sheila Glover (94b); Haverfordwest County AFC (47a); Haverfordwest Civic Society (22, 23b, 59a, 67a, 116b); Margaret Harries (51b, 80a); Mary Hay (96b); Stuart Hayden (42); Jack Holt (15b, 34b, 39b, 57a, 61a, 65, 68a, 69, 89, 96a); Ken and Viola Howell (6, 34a, 38a, 86b); Lyn Jenkins (30a, 44a); Sheila John (39a); Wyn Jones (49b, 113a); Arthur Kendrick (7); Tom Lamb (114a); Bob Livesey (84b); Peggy Munt, from the collection of Billy Munt (19a, 20a, 21b, 25a, 27a, 28b, 29a, 36b, 57b, 66b, 127); Bill Nicholas (26, 29b, 43a, 45, 56, 68b, 100a, 101a, 115, 116a, 118b, 120a, 121a); Evangeline Nisbet (60b, 112a); Gerald Oliver (8, 12, 15a, 61b, 62, 86a, 87a, 90b, 99, 101b, 102, 103b, 104, 105, 106a, 107, 108, 110b); Hugh Phillips (46b, 47b, 48b); from the Harold Price collection in the Pembrokeshire Record Office (18, 19b, 20b, 21a, 23a, 24b, 25b, 27b, 28a, 44b, 58, 63, 66a, 67b, 82b, 98b, 120b); Nancy Price (83b, 91a); Miss A.G. Rees (75); Derek Rees (118a); Bill Richards (50, 51a); Hilary Richards (17, 41); Anne Roberts and Margaret Walters (35b); Gladys Saies (78a, 114b); Mary Sinnett (43b, 70b); Joffre Swales (76, 77, 97, 117); Pat Swales-Barker (30b, 64, 90a, 91b); Maldwyn Thomas (2, 72a, 74b, 84a, 87b, 88a, 119a); Peggy Thomas (92, 93); Bill Thomas (79); David Tozer (49a); Barbara Tubb (71b, 72b, 73); Rosie Vaughan (53, 54a); Stephen Vincent-Davies (60a); Gwyn Warlow (95b, 98a); John and Glenys Warren (24a, 38b, 40, 110a, 113b); Peggy Watkins (81, 122b); Canon William Watkins (83a, 85a, 119b); Dilys Watts (52a); Alf Williams (112b); Bernard Williams (88b); Phyllis Williams (70a); Roger Worsley (4, 9, 10, 11, 13, 14, 16, 31, 35a, 36a, 37, 55, 82a, 100b, 103a, 109, 122a, 125b, 126).

The Society particularly acknowledges the permission given to select from the collections of Billy Munt and Harold Price, contemporaries and prominent members of the Haverfordwest Camera Club; and the extensive collection of Roger Worsley whose photographs, with their captions of the early days, are used widely throughout the book. Finally, the Society wishes to thank Mr Simon Eckley, Project Editor, for his help and encouragement during the book's compilation.